DARK SEAS

The Battle of Cape Matapan

BRITANNIA NAVAL HISTORIES OF WORLD WAR II

THIS EDITION IS PUBLISHED TO
COMMEMORATE THE OPENING OF
THE MARINE BUILDING BY
HRH PRINCE PHILIP ON
TUESDAY, 30 OCTOBER 2012 AT
PLYMOUTH UNIVERSITY

NUMBER 247/300

This edition first published in the United Kingdom in 2012 by
University of Plymouth Press, Portland Square, B322, Drake Circus,
Plymouth, Devon, PL4 8AA, United Kingdom.

Paperback   ISBN 978-1-84102 -304-5
Hardback   ISBN 978-1-84102-303-8

© University of Plymouth Press 2012

The rights of this work have been asserted in accordance with the Crown Copyright, Designs and Patents Act 1988.

A CIP catalogue record of this book is available from the British Library.

Publisher: Paul Honeywill
Series Editors: G. H. Bennett, J. E. Harrold and R. Porter
Commissioning Editor: Charlotte Carey
Publishing Assistant: Maxine Aylett

All rights reserved. No part of this publication may be reproduced, stored in a retrieval system or transmitted in any form or by any means whether electronic, mechanical, photocopying, recording, or otherwise, without the prior written permission of UPP. Any person who carries out any unauthorised act in relation to this publication may be liable to criminal prosecution and civil claims for damages.

Historical content courtesy of Britannia Museum, Britannia Royal Naval College, Dartmouth, TQ6 0HJ.

Cover image © Edward Stables 2012

Typeset by University of Plymouth Press in Janson 10/14pt.
Printed and bound by Short Run Press, Exeter, EX2 7LW, United Kingdom.

The historical documents reproduced here appear as unedited text, apart from minor changes made to date formats and corrections to typing errors found in the original.

Britannia Royal Naval College

A majestic landmark, which towers above the harbour town of Dartmouth in Devon, Britannia Royal Naval College was designed by royal architect Sir Aston Webb to project an image of British sea power. A fine example of Edwardian architecture, the College has prepared future generations of officers for the challenges of service and leadership since 1905.

The Britannia Museum opened in 1999 to safeguard the College's rich collection of historic artefacts, art and archives and promote greater public understanding of Britain's naval and maritime heritage, as a key element in the development of British history and culture. It also aims to instil a sense of identity and ethos in the Officer Cadets that pass through the same walls as their forbears, from great admirals to national heroes, to royalty.

Contents

Foreword	6
Introduction	10
Abbreviations	20
General Situation, March 1941	21
The Naval Situation, March 1941	23
The Commander-in-Chief's Plans	26
The Italian Fleet	29
Enemy Forces at Sea	30
British Fleet Movements	32
Commencement of Action	35
The C.-in-C.'s Movements, 28 March	38
HMS *Formidable*'s First Striking Force Takes Off	41
Action with the Italian Battleship	43
The First Attack on the *Vittorio Veneto*	44
Attack by Maleme Striking Force on the 3rd Division	46
Movements of the British Battle Fleet (Force A)	47
The *Formidable*'s Second Striking Force Awaits Orders	49
Position at 1330	50
The Second Attack on the *Vittorio Veneto*	51
RAF Bombers from Greece	52
The Pursuit 1330 – 1810	55
The Situation at 1915, 28 March	57
Third Torpedo Attack on the *Vittorio Veneto*	60
Movements of the British Battle Fleet	62
VALF and the Cruisers of Force B	63
Destroyer Striking Force	65
British Fleet Night Action	69
The Destroyers with HMAS *Stuart*	72
The Sinking of the *Zara* and *Pola*	76
Proceedings of Battle Fleet	77
Force D and Greek Destroyers	78

Italian Fleet	80
Events after 1500 on 28 March	88
The Return to Alexandria	92
The Commander-in-Chief's Comments	93
A Few Reflections	96
Appendix A	98
Appendix B	101
Appendix C	103
Appendix D	110
Appendix E	122
Appendix F	125
Appendix G	129
Appendix H	132
Appendix I	135
Appendix J	137
Appendix K	139
Endnotes	141
Biographies	147
Britannia Naval Histories of World War II Series	150

Foreword

HRH Prince Philip, Lord High Admiral

I was very interested to discover that the Britannia Museum, which I had opened in 1999 during my Term's 60th anniversary reunion, has embarked on a project to publish a series of Second World War battle summaries. As I had been a cadet at Dartmouth in 1939 and was present at the Battle of Matapan, it did not come as a great surprise when I was asked to write a foreword for the summary of the Battle.

I entered the Sandquay Barracks at the Britannia Royal Naval College in the spring of 1939 as a 'Special Entry' Cadet. As that time the normal age of entry to the College was 13. Special Entry meant that we had completed our School Certificate examinations at school, and then sat for the Civil Service entry examinations to qualify for entry into the Royal Navy. Previous Special Entry Cadets had gone straight to the training cruiser HMS *Vindictive*, where they were joined by senior Dartmouth Cadets. However, with the onset of war, she was taken back into general service, and my Term was sent to the Sandquay Barracks at Dartmouth instead. I completed my two terms at the College and was appointed to the First World War battleship, HMS *Ramillies*, and joined her in Colombo on 22 February 1940.

In January 1941, after Greece has been invaded by Italy, I was appointed to HMS *Valiant*, another WWI battleship, currently serving in the Mediterranean Fleet based in Alexandria. After a year of relative peace and quiet in the Indian Ocean, things certainly hotted-up in the Mediterranean. My introduction to the 'shooting war' was a bombardment of Bardia, when the Italian shore batteries shot back. This was followed by a convoy to Malta, when the carrier, HMS *Illustrious*, was damaged by Stuka dive bombers.

All this is on the record. What is not on the record is what it was like to be a Midshipman (the lowest form of life in the Navy) taking part in the Matapan campaign. Keeping everyone accurately informed of what was going on in a battleship, with a ship's company of 1,200 (including some 20 Midshipmen) was not really possible. Furthermore, all these events took place 70 years ago, and, as most elderly people have discovered, memories tend to fade – to put it mildly. Consequently, what follows needs to be treated as 'faction'.

Quite how information about what was going on percolated to the Gunroom is a mystery, but even the Midshipmen were becoming aware that the Italian fleet was thought to be at sea, and that there might be a chance of catching them. There was definitely a special atmosphere of anticipation of something dramatic in prospect when the Fleet put to sea from Alexandria during the night of 27 March.

My Action Station was on the bridge, and at night I had control of the port searchlight, so I managed to gather roughly what was going on by overhearing snippets of conversation from the compass platform. My impression was that an Italian battle fleet was at sea and was engaged in a fight with our light forces of cruisers and destroyers, which were attempting to lure the Italians towards our battleships. Then the carrier, HMS *Formidable* pulled out of the line to fly off a strike of Swordfish torpedo bombers. The general impression was that there might be the chance of catching the Italian heavy ships, provided they kept up their chase of our cruisers. Later, just before dusk, *Formidable* flew off another strike. It then transpired that the Italians had turned away after some of their ships had been hit by torpedoes from the Swordfish. The chase went on into a still, calm night, although it was apparent that our cruisers and destroyers were busy further north.

My recollection is that *Valiant* was the only capital ship fitted with, what is now known as RADAR, but was then known as RDF, and was therefore stationed immediately astern of HMS *Warspite*, Admiral Cunningham's Flagship. As far as I was concerned, it seemed that there was little chance of our catching up with the retreating Italians, and, as it got dark there was a general air of anti-climax. Then, suddenly, in the quiet of the night, came a report from our RDF operator that he had an echo on the port bow at about 5,000 yards of what appeared to be a stationary ship. I turned my searchlight on to the bearing given by the RDF operator in the hope of seeing the target. Just then the destroyer *Greyhound* turned her searchlight on which, I think, picked up an Italian destroyer, but the loom was enough for me to make out a ship on the horizon. I seem to remember that I reported that I had a target in sight, and was ordered to 'open shutter'. The beam lit up a stationary cruiser, but we were so close by then that the beam only lit up half the ship.

At this point all hell broke loose, as all our eight 15 inch guns, plus those of the Flagship and *Barham*'s started firing at the stationary cruiser, which disappeared in an explosion and a cloud of smoke. I was then ordered to 'train left' and lit up another Italian cruiser, which was given the same treatment. By this time the night was full of smoke, loud bangs and flashes and the dark shapes of our destroyers, with their coloured 'recognition lights', appeared and disappeared. That bit of the Mediterranean then became a very dangerous place. There must have been some twenty British and Italian warships dashing about in every direction at high speed. It was at this point the C.-in-C. ordered all ships not engaged in sinking the enemy to withdraw to the north east. Bangs and flashes went on for a bit, but then things gradually calmed down.

The next morning the battle fleet returned to the scene of the battle while attempts were made to pick up survivors. This was rudely interrupted by an attack by German bombers. Fortunately they missed, although *Valiant* was straddled diagonally from the port quarter to the starboard bow. A Royal Marine sentry on the quarterdeck was killed by a splinter, but otherwise no damage was done. Except that the two bombs going off virtually simultaneously, made the whole ship flex along its length. The only result was that some of the hatches in the armoured deck took some time to be forced open.

The return to Alexandria was uneventful, and the peace and quiet was much appreciated.

BUCKINGHAM PALACE

Introduction

Dr J. E. Harrold

The Battle for Cape Matapan stands out as the biggest and most decisive battle between surface fleets in the Mediterranean during World War II. It also stands out among the series of staff battle summaries concerning the theatre of operations in the Mediterranean by warranting a publication of its own. Written shortly after the war, the summary presents an initial review of the battle, drawing on the accounts of those present on both sides. As such, it provides the most detailed and vivid account of ship and aircraft movement as the enemy is hunted, trailed, avoided and engaged. It also conveys the 'fog of war' in which accurate intelligence combines with the inaccurate and misleading to paint an often confusing picture of events. Written so soon after the event, there is inevitably little reflection in the account, which is also rendered incomplete by the omission of the role played by ULTRA in enabling the British to read Italian and German signals. Its original 'restricted' classification meant it was only to be released to certain individuals, including select foreign governments and international organisations, but was not otherwise to be made generally available to the public. However, this summary presents a unique insight into one of the last fleet engagements in naval history and therefore warrants a wider readership.

Unlike the Atlantic, control of the Mediterranean was not a matter of national survival for Britain. However, since the opening of the Suez Canal in 1869 it had become a valuable lifeline between the United Kingdom and its dominions in Asia and Australasia, a significance reinforced as demand for Middle Eastern oil emerged. Moreover, its strategic importance as the major means of supply and communication with theatres of war from North Africa to the Middle East, the Balkans and Italy ensured that the fight for control of the Mediterranean would continue until the end of the war in Europe.

It was not until June 1940 that the Mediterranean became a major problem for Britain, caused by two seismic shifts in the war: the entry of Italy into the war followed only days later by the collapse of France. At once Britain had lost an ally and gained an enemy, the impact of which was most keenly felt in the Mediterranean. The Italian Navy (Regia Marina), under the command of Admiral Angelo Iachino, presented a formidable opponent; modern, well designed and generally faster than its older Royal Navy (RN) counterparts; it also had the advantage of being able to focus solely on the war in the Mediterranean while Britain and the Allies had to stretch resources to cover the Atlantic and later the Pacific. It had been designed principally to provide home defence against the French Navy, a role it was clearly not required to fulfil, and preferred to remain 'a fleet in being', reluctant to engage in battle, save for the protection of the occasional convoy, while continuing to pose a sizeable threat to its opponents.[1] The apparent reluctance of the Regia Marina to engage in battle was in part due to its limited supply of fuel.[2] When it did venture out it suffered other significant deficiencies, notably the lack of organic (sea-launched) aircraft, the absence of radar and the centralised land-based command of the Italian Naval Headquarters (Supermarina), which denied Italian commanders the freedom of action enjoyed by their British counterparts. All these factors were to weigh against the Regia Marina when it met the RN at Cape Matapan.

By comparison, the British Mediterranean Fleet, which included the Australian light cruiser HMAS *Perth* and the destroyer HMAS *Stuart*, under the command of Admiral Sir Andrew Cunningham (know as ABC) began the war smaller[3] and older. All three battleships engaged at Matapan, HMS *Warspite*, *Valiant* and *Barham* had been present at the Battle of Jutland, 25 years earlier. Crucially, each but *Barham*, together with other more modern British ships, was fitted with radar. The RN also enjoyed the presence of an aircraft carrier, although by the time the two fleets met at Matapan it had already been necessary to replace one carrier, the damaged HMS *Illustrious*, with *Formidable*. The ensuing battle would be 'the first time that carrier-borne aircraft played a vital and indispensable role in a main fleet action'.[4] A further advantage would also present itself at Matapan; the legacy of pre-war night-fighting training. Indeed Cunningham could claim to be 'arguably the most expert 'night-fighter' in the Royal Navy', while the Italians neither expected nor prepared for action after dark.[5]

Initial engagements between the two fleets had been largely inconclusive, the Regia Marina preferring a safe escape to open battle. However, there could be no escape when, assisted by long-range American built photo-reconnaissance aircraft, the British targeted the Italian naval base at Taranto on the evening of 11 November 1940, with the aim of reducing the Italian threat to essential convoys from Malta to troops in North Africa. The attack, conducted by Fairey Swordfish torpedo bombers from HMS *Illustrious*, severely damaged two battleships and sank a third; arguably the psychological impact was as devastating as the material one on the

Italian fleet. The RN now enjoyed superiority in capital ships; however, it remained outnumbered in lesser classes; 'command of the sea' was still far from secured.[6]

Ashore, Mussolini was attempting to assert Italian military might. Using the previously invaded and occupied Albania as a springboard, Italian forces invaded Greece on 28 October 1940. Unfortunately for the Italian dictator, his adventure rapidly and vividly highlighted the fallacy of his ambition to reclaim the glory of the Roman Empire; not until the intervention of German forces did Greece eventually fall. The invasion of Greece also provoked Britain to become involved, the government deciding to send an expeditionary force of Commonwealth troops from North Africa to the new front in Greece. This was a commitment the British could ill afford and was arguably intended as much to demonstrate, particularly to the still neutral USA, their resolve to continue to fight the Axis powers.[7] The safe passage of men and material from Alexandria to Greece would place further responsibility on Cunningham's fleet which, since Germany's increased presence in-theatre, was also required to deal with the threat posed by the German bombers of Fliegerkorps X, recently arrived from Norway.

It was against this background that the characteristically cautious Supermarina would order Admiral Iachino to take his fleet to sea. The reasons for this decision were summarised by the Deputy Chief of Staff of the Navy, Admiral Campioni as: "(i) the volume of shipping between Egypt and Greece; (ii) the need to allow the Navy to go into action; and (iii) the pressure from the Germans".[8] Of all these imperatives it is the latter which appeared decisive; as Iachino himself is quoted in the Battle Summary, the German instance on offensive cruises in the Eastern Mediterranean "was in the final analysis the determining cause of our operation at the end of March".[9]

The Supermarina's plan was to intercept British convoys to the north and south of the island of Crete, thus disrupting their route for resupply from North Africa to Greece. This would involve a formidable fleet of one battleship, six heavy cruisers, two light cruisers and 13 destroyers. The battleship *Vittorio Veneto*, in which Iachino flew his flag, was so new that it had avoided destruction at Taranto and boasted nine 15-in guns and a top speed of 30 knots. The only omission was of air cover and reconnaissance; this was promised by the Luftwaffe although in reality it failed to materialise properly. The fleet left Naples on 26 March, encouraged by German intelligence reports that the British could muster just one battleship and no operational aircraft carrier, since *Illustrious* had been bombed by German planes in Malta harbour. The reality was that the British had in fact three operational battleships and the aircraft carrier *Formidable* had arrived on station earlier in March.

According to the Battle Summary, it was at 1220 on 27 March that an RAF Sunderland Flying Boat reported a force of enemy cruisers, which subsequently persuaded Cunningham to proceed to sea himself.[10] However, it is now known that ULTRA decryptions of German and Italian signals had already alerted the British to the Regia Marina's intentions; the deployment of a reconnaissance plane in clear view of the Italians being intended to deflect any suspicions among the enemy that their signals were being read.[11] Forewarned, Cunningham had subtly suspended all but one convoy sailing, allowing his forces to focus on searching for the enemy. Meanwhile, despite the loss of surprise Iachino was ordered to continue, although he was now to concentrate his forces south of Crete and sweep north past Cape Matapan. For the Supermarina the political imperative to engage the British outweighed any military considerations.[12]

The proceeding Battle Summary provides the most comprehensive account of ship and aircraft movements from 27 to 29 March and therefore does not require repeating here. However, given the complications and intricacies of the engagement an overview of the battle is nonetheless useful. The British fleet was divided into two main Forces. Cunningham led the battleship squadron, based at Alexandria and composed of the three battleships, a carrier and four destroyers. The second cruiser and destroyer force, based at Piraeus (Greece) was led by Vice Admiral Pridham-Wippell, referred to throughout the summary as Vice Admiral Light forces (VALF). Two additional forces constituted a further flotilla of destroyers and two submarines. The Regia Marina was similarly divided into two cruiser/destroyer forces and the *Vittorio Veneto* battle group.

The VALF set out first to hunt for evidence that the Regia Marina was at sea; by 27 March it became apparent that it was and that evening, unnoticed by the Italians and Germans, Cunningham's fleet departed Alexandria to rendezvous with Pridham-Wippell. The first positive sighting of the enemy came around 0745/28 when Vice-Admiral Sansonetti's cruiser force spotted the VALF and opened fire. Knowing himself to be outgunned Pridham-Wippell altered course in an attempt to draw his opponent towards the big guns of Cunningham's battle fleet. After an hour of gunfire and chasing, Iachino, suspicious of the British retreat ordered his own ships to join the *Vittorio Veneto* battle fleet in a similar attempt to lure his enemy towards greater fire-power; he was still unaware of Cunningham's ever closer presence at sea. By the time of the next encounter at 1050 VALF was trapped between Iachino's and Sansonetti's forces. Pridham-Wippell's only option was again to beat a hasty retreat behind clouds of smoke. Relief finally arrived at 1127 in the shape of a group of Albacore torpedo bombers, originally launched from *Formidable* in an attempt to slow down the faster Italian ships. Without air cover of his own, Iachino had little choice other than to turn for home waters. *Vittorio Veneto* had not been hit on this occasion; however, a second strike from the carrier, conducted between 1510–1525 proved more effective, with one torpedo hitting the battleship, causing it to stop temporarily and take on water. The price of this strike was the loss of the attacking aircraft and its crew of three, including the squadron leader Lieutenant Commander J. Dalyell Stead RN; remarkably these were to be the only losses suffered by the British during the battle. However, it was not long before Iachino was underway again, albeit at a much slower rate of knots. Meanwhile land-based RAF bombers from Greece and Fleet Air Arm bombers from Crete also joined in the attacks, but to little effect. A third and final strike launched from *Formidable* met with more success, hitting the heavy cruiser *Pola* and causing her to stop dead in the water; the significance of this hit was to prove far greater than could initially have been imagined. An hour later, onboard *Vittorio Veneto*, Iachino, unaware of the relative proximity of British ships, finally made the fateful decision to send Vice Admiral Cattaneo with the cruisers *Zara* and *Fiume* and four destroyers to assess *Pola*'s situation and render assistance as necessary. Iachino's motives for making this decision are considered in some detail in the Battle Summary, for it was to turn the events of the following night from tragedy to disaster for the *Regia Marina*.[13]

Meanwhile, disappointed to have missed the Italian flagship yet again, Cunningham had despatched eight destroyers, led by Captain P. J. Mack in *Jervis*, to continue the hunt. It had now become clear to the British Commander-in-Chief that if he was to engage the enemy with minimal risk to his own ships he would have to attack at night to avoid heavy aerial bombardment from land-based aircraft from Sicily. However, as the destroyers and VALF both continued to close in on the *Vittorio Veneto*, Cunningham's battle fleet came across Cattaneo's rescue party. With *Pola* fixed on *Valiant*'s radar, Cattaneo's ships were sighted close by; the battleships opened fire at such a range, Cunningham remarked, that "even a gunnery officer cannot miss".[14] That they were able to do so was in no small part due to the searchlights from the British ships that illuminated their targets. One of these searchlights, midship on *Valiant*, was manned by a young Prince Philip, whose dedication to his duty earned him a mention in despatches.[15] Soon after, *Zara*, *Fiume* and the destroyer *Alfieri* were all fatally hit. *Fiume* sank shortly after while *Zara*, *Alfieri* and the destroyer *Carducci* were later finished off by RN and RAN destroyers from Cunningham's escort group, the battleships having withdrawn to safety. Finally, having removed survivors, the stricken *Pola* was sunk by two torpedoes.

Meanwhile, Mack and Pridham-Wippell had continued their pursuit of *Vittorio Veneto*; however the chase was unintentionally lost when VALF responded to Cunningham's signal for all forces not engaged in sinking the enemy to retire north eastwards to avoid attack from the Luftwaffe once daylight returned. The next day (30 March) the British Mediterranean Fleet returned safely to port having dealt a devastating blow to the Regia Marina's surface fleet: for the loss of just one British aircraft and its three-man crew the Italians had lost three heavy cruisers, and two destroyers; their newest battleship had suffered significant damage while some 3,000 men had been killed, injured or captured. Nevertheless, in Cunningham's final analysis, quoted in the Summary: "The results of the action cannot be viewed with entire satisfaction since the damaged *Vittorio Veneto* was allowed to escape".[16]

Certainly the war for control of the Mediterranean was far from won and the Royal Navy and its allies would continue to suffer devastating losses. But these losses would be at the hands of aircraft and submarines. Had the Regia Marina's surface fleet survived, Allied casualties could only have been greater, not least during the subsequent evacuations from Crete and Greece. The failure of such operations could have proved fatal for the future of campaigns around the Mediterranean. By the time of the Battle of El Alamein in October – November 1942, the British Eighth Army was better armed and better supplied than Rommel's Afrika Korps, despite a considerably longer supply route.[17] It may be a truism but ultimately a war between nations can only be won on land. A war can, however, be lost at sea when the survival of peoples and their fighting forces is dependent upon safe and open access to the seas.

References

1. Hough, R. (1999), *Naval Battles of the Twentieth Century*, Constable, London, pp.120-121.
2. Greene J. & Massignani, A. (1998), *The Naval War in the Mediterranean 1940–1943*, Chatham Publishing, London, pp.143-144. Provides a detailed examination of Italian fuel supplies and their impact on Italian operations; ultimately it is impossible to know if the Regia Marina would have ventured out more if there had been a greater supply of fuel available.
3. See following Battle Summary, for ratio of RN/RAN to Regia Marina ships.
4. Pack, S. W. C. (1961), *The Battle of Matapan*, B.T. Batsford Ltd, London, p.7.
5. Goldrick, J. 'Cunningham: Matapan, 1941.' In Grove, E. (ed.) (1994) *Great Battles of the Royal Navy as Commemorated in the Gunroom*, Britannia Royal Naval College, Dartmouth, Bramley Books, London, p.198.
6. Brown, D. (2001), *The Royal Navy and the Mediterranean. Vol. II November 1940–December 1941*, Frank Cass, London, p.xiv.
7. Hough, R. (1999), *Naval Battles of the Twentieth Century*, Constable, London, p.123.
8. Greene, J. & Massignani, A. (1998), *The Naval War in the Mediterranean 1940–1943*, Chatham Publishing, London, p.146.
9. See following Battle Summary. The Admiral is also quoted complaining at not been consulted with regard to the preceding Italo-German naval conference held at Merano, 13–14 February.
10. See following Battle Summary.
11. Greene, J. & Massignani, A. (1998), *The Naval War in the Mediterranean 1940–1943*, Chatham Publishing, London, pp.159-160. It was widely suspected by the Italians that the loss of the element of surprise was due to the presence of a traitor.
12. Scalzo, A. M. (2001): *Battle of Cape Matapan: World War II Italian Naval Massacre*, www.historynet.com./battle-of-cape-matapan-world-war-ii-italian-naval-massacre.htm.
13. See following Battle Summary.

14. Goldrick, J. 'Cunningham: Matapan, 1941' in Grove, E. (ed.) (1994) *Great Battles of the Royal Navy as Commemorated in the Gunroom*, Britannia Royal Naval College, Dartmouth, Bramley Books, London, p.203.
15. Brandreth, G. (2004), *Philip and Elizabeth: Portrait of a Marriage*, Century, London, p.152-153.
16. See following Battle Summary.
17. Macintyre, D. (1964), *The Battle for the Mediterranean*, B.T. Batsford Ltd, London, p.15.

Bibliography

Brandreth, G. (2004), *Philip and Elizabeth: Portrait of a Marriage*, Century, London.

Brown, D. (2001), *The Royal Navy and the Mediterranean. Vol. II November 1940–December 1941*, Frank Cass, London.

Goldrick, J. 'Cunningham: Matapan, 1941' in Grove, E. (ed.) (1994), *Great Battles of the Royal Navy as Commemorated in the Gunroom*, Britannia Royal Naval College, Dartmouth, Bramley Books, London.

Greene, J. & Massignani, A. (1998), *The Naval War in the Mediterranean 1940-1943*, Chatham Publishing, London.

Grove, E. (ed.) (1994), *Great Battles of the Royal Navy as Commemorated in the Gunroom*, Britannia Royal Naval College, Dartmouth. Bramley Books, London.

Holloway A. (1993), *From Dartmouth to War: A Midshipman's Journal*, Bucklands Publications Ltd, London.

Hough, R. (1999), *Naval Battles of the Twentieth Century*, Constable, London.

Macintyre, D. (1964), *The Battle for the Mediterranean*, B.T. Batsford Ltd, London.

Pack, S. W. C. (1961), *The Battle of Matapan*, B.T. Batsford Ltd, London.

Scalzo, A. M. (2001), *Battle of Cape Matapan: World War II Italian Naval Massacre*, www.historynet.com./battle-of-cape-matapan-world-war-ii-italian-naval-massacre.htm.

BR. 1736 (35)   Restricted

NAVAL STAFF HISTORY
SECOND WORLD WAR
BATTLE SUMMARY No. 44

THE BATTLE OF CAPE MATAPAN
28 March, 1941

This book is the property of His Majesty's Government and is for the use of persons in His Majesty's Service only. It must not be shown, or made available to, the Press or to any member of the public.

T.S.D. 72/49
Tactical and Staff Duties Division (Historical Section),
Naval Staff, Admiralty, S.W.1

ABBREVIATIONS

A.A.	Anti-Aircraft.
A/C	Aircraft.
A.P.C.	Armour-Piercing, Capped.
A/S	Anti-Submarine.
A.S.V.	Anti-Surface Vessel (Airborne Radar Set).
A.T.O.	Assisted Take-Off (Launching Gear For A/C).
B/S	Battleship.
C.S.	Cruiser Squadron.
D.F.	Destroyer Flotilla.
D/F	Direction Finding (From W/T Reception).
E.B.I.	Evershed Bearing Indicator.
F.A.A.	Fleet Air Arm.
F/B	Flying Boat.
G.A.B.	General Alarm Bearing.
H.E.	High Explosive.
R.A. (A)	Rear-Admiral, Aircraft Carrier.
RAF	Royal Air Force.
S.A.P.	Semi-Armour-Piercing (R.A.F. Bombs).
T/B (A/C)	Torpedo-Bomber.
T.O.O.	Time Of Origin.
T.B.R (A/C)	Torpedo-Bomber-Reconnaissance.
T.S.R (A/C)	Torpedo Spotting Reconnaissance.
VALF	Vice-Admiral Of Light Forces.

General Situation, March 1941

In June 1940 the sudden collapse of France and the entry of Italy into the war gravely compromised the British situation in the Mediterranean. These events were followed in October 1940 by Mussolini's treacherous attack on Greece with a view to gaining control over the Eastern Mediterranean. He met with an unexpected set-back and in January 1941 the Italian forces were falling back on Valona in Albania. Germany was already preparing to enter the lists. On 1 March, 1941 Bulgaria signed the Three Power Pact complying with Hitler's demand to allow twenty fully mechanised German divisions to enter Bulgaria and take post along the Yugoslav frontier, a very evident warning of a German attack on Greece.

A lull had occurred in the Libyan Campaign. Tobruk and Benghazi had been captured from the Italians in January and the British Government decided to send two infantry divisions (one Australian and one New Zealand) and an armoured brigade from Libya to assist Greece in the impending attack. On 2 March, Mr. Eden, Secretary of State for War, and General Sir John Dill, C.I.G.S., were in Athens conferring with the Greek Government. The transfer of this force (Operation 'Lustre'), which began to move on 4 March, absorbed for a time all the energies of the Mediterranean fleet. Its transport required, during March and April, 27 escorted convoys (15 northbound and 12 southbound) between Egypt and Greece, while the forces disembarked numbered 58,364 personnel and 8,588 vehicles, guns and tanks.

Enemy air forces were active; Italian submarines were on the move; mines laid by air in the Suez Canal blocked the passage of the *Formidable* on her way through the Red Sea to the Mediterranean to replace the *Illustrious* and she did not reach Port Said until 9 March. It is satisfactory to note that in spite of attacks by air and submarine not a soldier was lost on the way to Greece. Italian submarines failed to stop the convoys and one of them (the *Anfitrite*) attacking a convoy from the Aegean was sunk by the *Greyhound* on 6 March; but behind the submarines lay the Italian fleet, which might at any moment appear on the Aegean route. It is in the light of these circumstances that the Battle of Matapan was fought for nothing less than the control of the Eastern Mediterranean and all the vast commitments dependent upon it.

The Naval Situation, March 1941

In the nine months that had passed since Italy entered the war the Italian fleet had made very few major sorties, of which two led to running fights with out Fleet, viz.: the action off Calabria on 9 July, 1940 (Battle Summary No. 8) and the action off Cape Spartivento on 27 November, 1940 (Battle Summary No. 9). Both of these encounters had ended in dismal retreat. On another occasion, 30 September 1940, their retreat took place before action was possible, although their preponderance of force, i.e., battleships 5 to 2, cruisers 11 to 5, destroyers more than 2 to 1 might have tempted them to an encounter (Naval Staff History (Med.), Vol. I, Sec. 86[1]). Furthermore, they had submitted tamely to the attack on Taranto (11 November, 1940), the bombardment of Valona (18 December, 1940), the bombardment of Bardia (3 January, 1941), the passage of a through convoy from Gibraltar to Greece on 7–10 January, 1941, and the bombardment of Genoa (9 February, 1941). What finally stirred them into action were the prospects of a great Spring offensive in the Balkans and the urgency of German protests.[2] Signs of increasing activity became apparent about 25 March. There was increasing aerial reconnaissance to the south and west of Greece and Crete, accompanied by daily attempts to reconnoitre Alexandria harbour, and other indications all pointing to some prospective action by the Italian fleet.

In the opinion of the C.-in-C. this action might take one of three forms: (1) attack on the British convoy routes in the Aegean with the despatch of an Italian convoy to the Dodecanese; (2) a diversion to cover a landing in Cyrenaica or Greece; (3) an attack on Malta. The most vulnerable target, in his opinion, was to be found in the British convoys to Greece, whose passage had to be safeguarded at all costs.

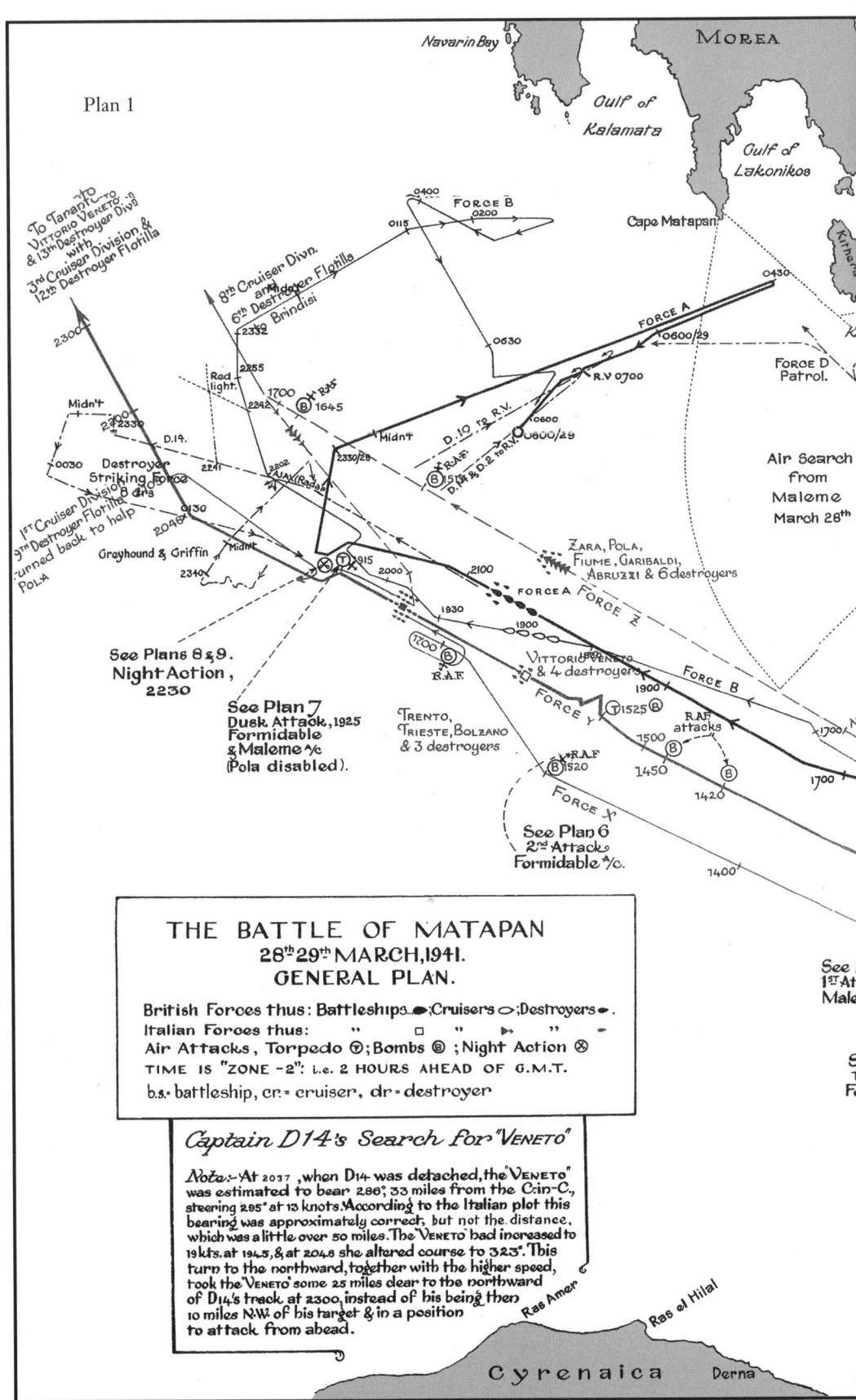

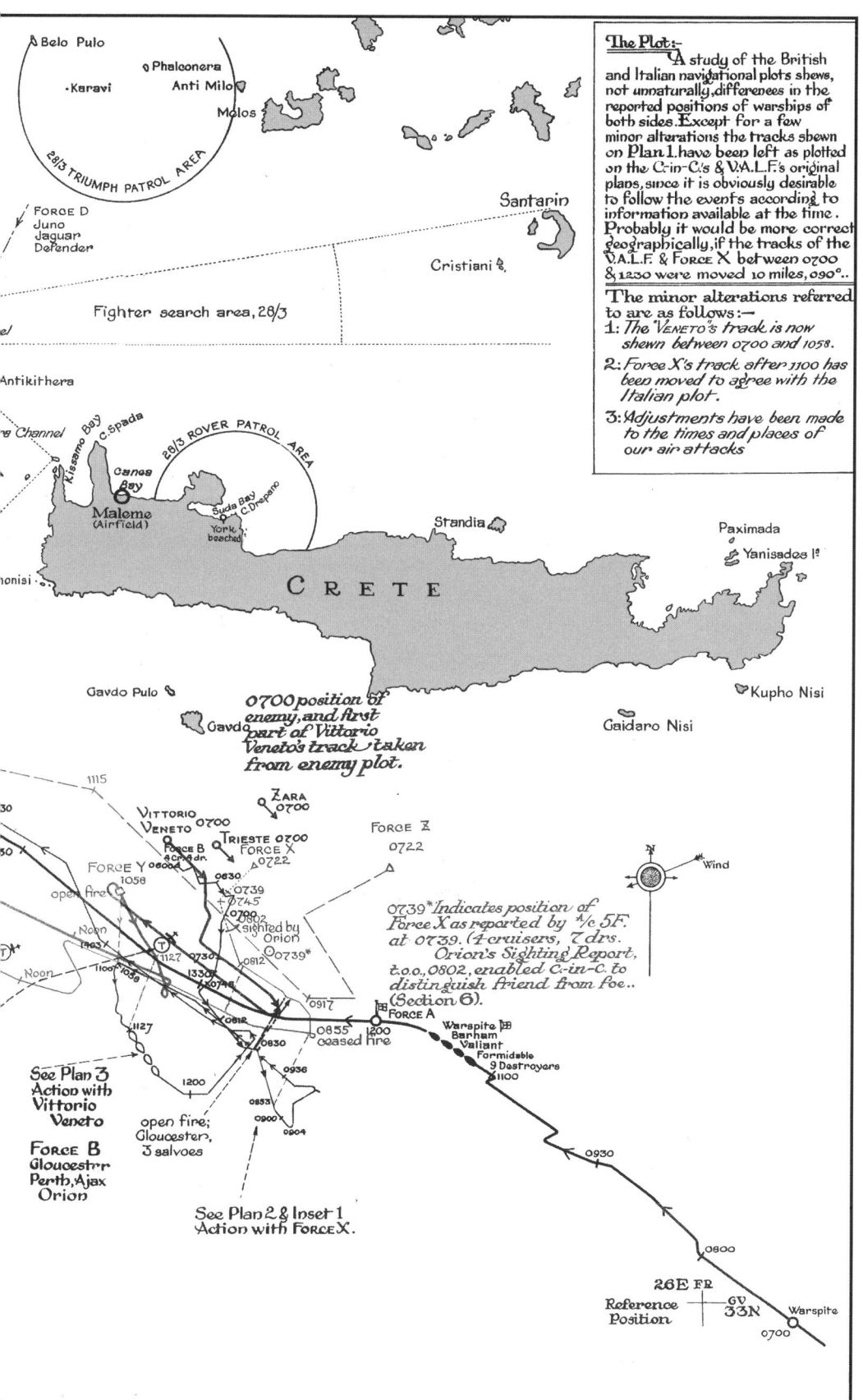

The Commander-in-Chief's Plans

The threat from enemy surface ships might be met by moving our battle fleet into the area west of Crete, but from that area it would sooner or later be bound to return to harbour for fuel, leaving the enemy free to attack. The C.-in-C. therefore decided to clear merchant shipping out of the area between Crete and Egypt for a time, and to dispose all his available forces to bring the enemy to action.

As it was important, however, to avoid arousing his suspicions and it was hoped that convoys in the Aegean would draw the Italians out, one convoy was left at sea – A.G.9,[3] bound north for the Piraeus. This was a troop convoy of six ships which had sailed from Egypt on 26 March with an escort of three British destroyers and a Greek flotilla leader. It was ordered to turn south at nightfall on 27 March so as to be eastward of the battle fleet at daylight 28 March. The sailing of a southbound convoy (G.A.8)[4] from the Piraeus was cancelled at the same time and the authorities in the Aegean were warned to keep the area clear of all shipping. The battle fleet was to proceed to sea from Alexandria under cover of night on the evening of 27 March.

The British fleet[5] was organised in four groups as follows:–

Force A Battle fleet	*Warspite* (Flag of Admiral Sir Andrew Cunningham, C.-in-C.), *Barham*, *Valiant*, *Formidable*.
Force A Destroyers (14th flotilla)	*Jervis* (Captain D.14), *Janus*, *Mohawk*, *Nubian*.

Force B Cruisers	*Orion* (Flag of Vice-Admiral Pridham-Wippell, Vice-Admiral, Light Forces), *Ajax*, *Perth*, *Gloucester*.
Force B Destroyers (2nd flotilla)	*Ilex* (Captain D.2), *Hasty*, *Hereward*, *Vendetta*.
Force C Destroyers (10th flotilla)	*Stuart* (Captain D.10), *Greyhound*, *Griffin*, *Hotspur*, *Havock*.
Force D[6]	*Juno*, *Jaguar*, *Defender*. Submarines *Rover* and *Triumph*.

Orders for appropriate disposition of the cruisers and destroyers were issued on 26 March as follows:

(a) Force B, consisting of 4 cruisers and 4 destroyers under Vice-Admiral, Light Forces, was to be S.W. of Gavdo Island, Crete, at daylight 28 March.
(b) Force C, consisting of 5 destroyers (*Stuart, Greyhound, Griffin, Hotspur, Havock*) was to join the VALF at that time.
(c) The T.S.R. squadrons (F.A.A.) in Crete and Cyrenaica were to be reinforced.
(d) The R.A.F. in Greece was requested to do its utmost with reconnaissance and bombing aircraft in the Aegean and to the west of Crete on 28 March.
(e) H.M. submarines *Rover* and *Triumph* were to patrol in the Aegean off Suda Bay and Milo respectively.
(f) Force D, consisting of 3 destroyers (*Juno, Jaguar* and *Defender*) at the Piraeus, was to be at short notice.
(g) The cruiser *Carlisle* was to proceed to Suda Bay, in Crete, to augment the A.A. defences there.
(h) The Greek naval forces were warned to be at short notice. This disposition was adopted with the intention of countering a possible cruiser raid into the Aegean. "It was designed to give flexibility and allowed for a quick change of plan if more intelligence came to hand."

Of the Fleet Air Arm, 37 aircraft[7] were available, viz.: A/c
(1) HMS *Formidable*. 13 Fulmars (803 and 806 Sqdns.),
   10 Albacores (826 and 829 Sqdns.) and 4 Swordfish. 27
(2) Royal Naval Air Station, Maleme, Crete.
   5 Swordfish (815 Sqdn.) 5
(3) Catapult aircraft (700 Sqdn.).
   2 Swordfish in *Warspite*; 2 Swordfish in *Valiant*;
   1 Walrus in *Gloucester* <u>5</u>
   <u>37</u>

The R.A.F., at the request of the C.-in-C., ordered the following aircraft to be held in readiness in Greece:

At Menidil[8] aerodrome	12 Blenheims,	No. 84 Sqdn.
	12 Blenheims,	No. 113 Sqdn.
At Paramythia[9] aerodrome	6 Blenheims,	No. 211 Sqdn.

These were armed with 500 lb. and 250 lb. S.A.P. Bombs. In addition, 201 Group R.A.F. undertook reconnaissance of the area of operations with Sunderland flying boats working from Malta and Alexandria.

The Italian Fleet

The effective strength of the Italian battle fleet at this period was estimated as three battleships fit for service, viz.: *Vittorio Veneto*, *G. Cesare* and *A. Doria*, the other three not having yet been repaired after damage sustained in the Fleet Air Arm attack on Taranto in November 1940. Of cruisers a strong force was available, namely seven 8-in. and at least nine 6-in. ships, whilst the number of Italian destroyers seems to have been at least double that of the British. In submarines the advantage was also heavily on the Italian side. With regard to air forces, the enemy, heavily reinforced by the German Luftwaffe, was in a very strong position and the area to the westward of Crete was well within bombing range of his aerodromes in Sicily, Southern Italy and the Dodecanese.

The Italian fleet[10] was organised as follows:

(1) Battleships (Force Y[11]), *Vittorio Veneto* (Flag, Admiral Iachino), and four destroyers (13th flot.).
(2) 1st Cruiser Division (Force Z[11]), *Zara*, *Fiume*, *Pola* and four destroyers (9th flot.).
(3) 3rd Cruiser Division (Force X[11]), *Trento*, *Trieste*, *Bolzano* and three destroyers (12th flot.).
(4) 8th Cruiser Division, *Giuseppe Garibaldi*, *Duea Di Abruzzi* and two destroyers (6th flot.).

The Italian forces, consisting of one battleship, eight cruisers and thirteen destroyers left their various ports on 26 March and, making junction at a rendezvous east of Syracuse, proceeded to the south-east (See pages 80-87).

Enemy Forces at Sea

At 1220 on 27 March, a British Flying Boat on reconnaissance reported a force of enemy cruisers[12] and a destroyer off Sicily in 36° 54' N., 17° 10' E. steering 120°, but owing to bad visibility was unable to shadow.

On the strength of this report the C.-in-C., Admiral Sir Andrew Cunningham, decided to proceed to sea. Finding, however, that the original dispositions would leave the cruisers without sufficient support and the battle fleet without sufficient destroyers for a screen, he made the following alterations in his plans:

(a) The VALF with the cruisers (Force B) was to rendezvous at 0630/28 further to the eastward, S. of Gavdo Is., in 34° 20' N., 24° 10' E.
(b) The five destroyers of Force C were to remain with the battle fleet.
(e) The movement of T.B.R. aircraft to Cyrenaica was cancelled.
(d) R.A.F. reconnaissance was arranged for 28 March over the South Ionian Sea, the South West Aegean and south of Crete.

The British main fleet (Force A), consisting of three battleships, one aircraft carrier and nine destroyers, left Alexandria at 1900/27 and as dusk fell, shrouding its departure, steered westward on a course 300°, at 20 knots. Six hours before, the VALF, Vice-Admiral Pridham-Wippell, had left the Piraeus (Athens) at 1300/27, with four cruisers and two destroyers, having ordered the remaining two destroyers to leave Suda Bay and join his flag in 34° 20' N., 24° 10' E., 30 miles south of Gavdo Island, south of Crete, at 0630/28.

The three destroyers of Force D were assembled at the Piraeus on the morning of 28 March[13] and after refuelling kept steam at short notice.

Instructions had already been given to the submarines *Rover* and *Triumph* and these were now amplified; they were ordered to patrol off Suda Bay and Anti Milo and wait for an enemy force or convoy expected to be entering the Aegean on 28 March. A message was also sent at 1822 to Captain Portal, Senior Officer at Suda Bay, warning him to withdraw patrols. Unfortunately that very morning his ship, the cruiser HMS *York*, had been attacked and hit by a new type of one-man motor explosive boat[14] and was lying badly damaged and beached in Suda Bay, a mishap which seriously affected British signal communications with the Fleet Air Arm force at Maleme.

British Fleet Movements

At 0400/28 the C.-in-C. with Force A, on a course of 310° at 16 knots, was in 32° 22' N., 27° 12' E., roughly 205 miles from the rendezvous of the cruiser force. The latter at 0600/28, steering to the south-east at 18 knots, sighted an enemy aircraft, identified later as an R.O.43. This type, used chiefly with catapults, indicated the presence of surface ships, and accordingly VALF as soon as *Ilex* and *Hasty* joined his screen, turned at 0645 to 200°, away from the direction of probable reconnaissance.

Meanwhile the *Formidable*, an hour before, at 0555, in 32° 44' N., 26° 57' E., had flown off a number of aircraft, A/S and fighters, to search the area between Crete and Cyrenaica as far west as longitude 23° E.

An air search had started even earlier from Maleme, in Crete, where four T.B.Rs. armed with torpedoes took off at 0445 to search to the west of Crete. One of them experienced engine trouble and had to jettison its torpedo and return; the others continued in company and, sighting nothing, returned at 0845.

It was 0720 when the enemy was first sighted south of Crete by aircraft 5B of HMS *Formidable*, which at 0722 amplified her report of four cruisers and four destroyers in 34° 22' N., 24° 47' E., steering 230°. The next report was made by *Formidable*'s aircraft, 5F at 0739, which announced four[15] cruisers and six destroyers, course 220° in 34° OS' N., 24° 26' E. (see Appendix D). These were part of the Italian Fleet, which at 0800 was south of Gavdo Island (Crete), steering 130°. It was disposed in three groups, termed by us Forces Z, X and Y as follows :–

Force Z[16]	i.e. (1st Cruiser Division, 3 *Zara* cruisers and (first sighted 0722, 8th Cruiser Division, 2 *Garibaldi* cruisers). A/C B)
Force X[16]	i.e. 3rd Cruiser Division, 3 *Trieste* cruisers. (first sighted 0739, A/C F)
Force Y[16]	*Vittorio Veneto*. (first sighted 1058 by VALF)

DARK SEAS

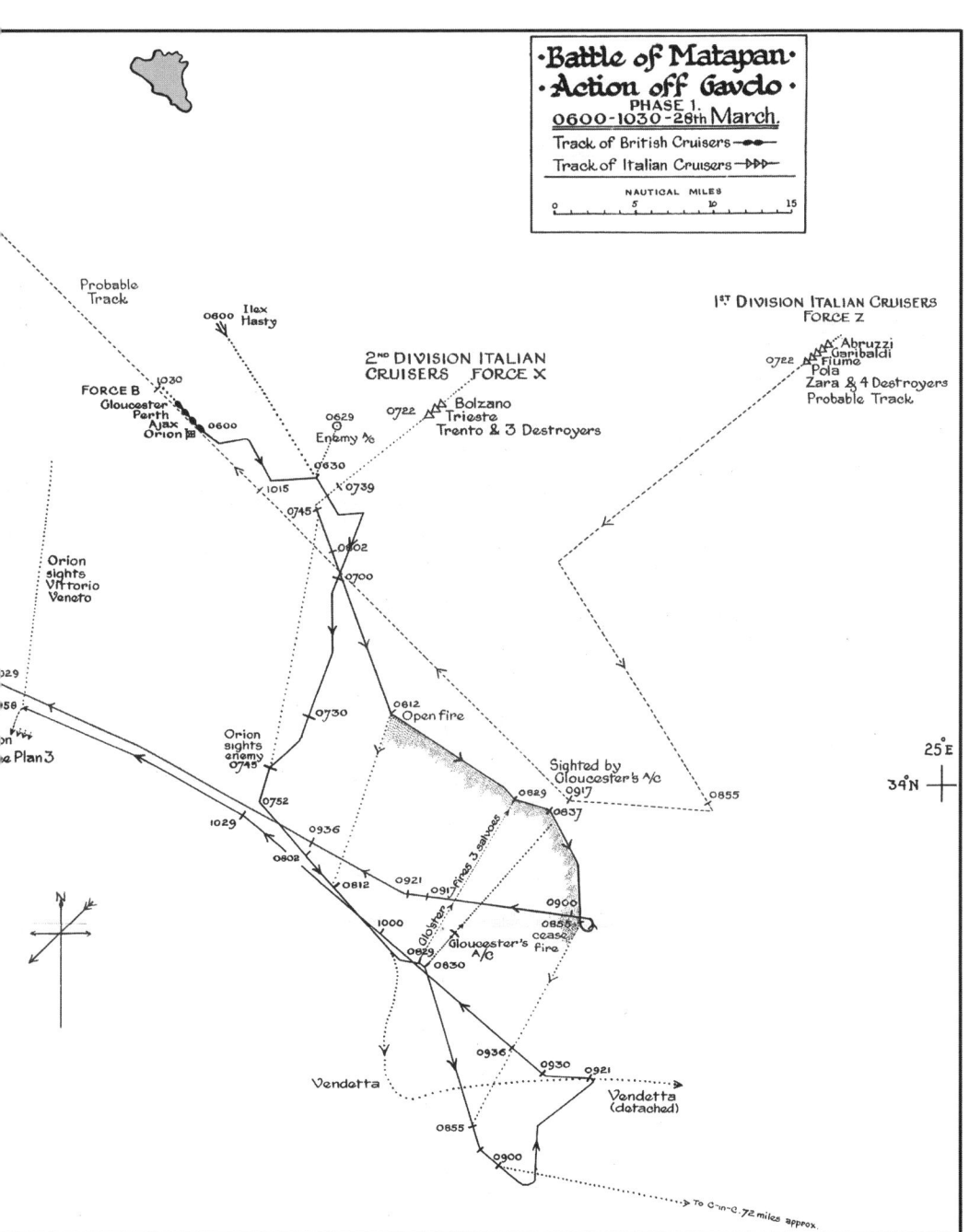

Plan 2

As the force first reported by aircraft 5B at 0722 was identical in composition with the British Cruiser Force B and was only some 35 miles north-east of it, it seemed to the VALF and to the C.-in-C. that Force B (British) had been mistaken for the enemy, and the C.-in-C. asked R.A. (A) whether his aircraft knew the position of our cruisers. When the second report came in, only 25 miles from the position of the first, it seemed again that it might be referring to our own cruisers. In actual fact the two air reports referred to two separate enemy cruiser forces, some 25 miles apart. One (designated Force X in Plan 1) was some 15 miles north of VALF; the other (designated Force Z) was some 30 miles north-east of him. The uncertainty was soon resolved for at 0745 the *Orion* (flagship) sighted smoke astern bearing 010° and a minute later identified enemy ships, which belonged to enemy Force X. It was then 0746.

Commencement of Action
(Plan 2)

When 25 miles south of Gavdo at 0600/28 March and on a S.E.'ly course the VALF – as already noted – had sighted an enemy aircraft and, after the *Ilex* and *Hasty* had joined his screen, turned at 0645 to course 200°, speed 20 knots, with the intention of avoiding further enemy air reconnaissance. The 0739 enemy report from the *Formidable*'s A/C 'F' was still being studied by VALF at 0745 when the *Orion* sighted the enemy astern, and at 0752 the VALF altered course to 140° and increased speed to 23 knots. Shortly afterwards (0755) the ships astern were seen to be three cruisers with some destroyers, and speed was increased to 28 knots. Suspecting them to be 8-in. cruisers of the *Zara* class, which were faster than his own and could outrange them, he decided to try to draw them towards our battleships, some 90 miles to the eastward. At 0802 he reported their position[17] and his own. Though not aware of it at the time he was "very uncomfortably placed" with a second powerful enemy cruiser squadron (Force Z) out of sight to the north-east in a position to cut him off from our battle fleet; also, the *Vittorio Veneto* was some 16 miles on his port quarter, steering S.E. His first enemy report was amplified at 0812 and simultaneously the enemy (3rd Division) opened fire, range 25,000 yards. Admiral Iachino comments on the opening range:

> "The *Trieste* Division opened fire at 22,000 metres and the first salvoes fell very short... the distance between the two groups was in fact never less than 24,000 metres (i.e., 27,000 yards). Atmospheric conditions were most unfavourable for range finding at great distance, especially with the old range finders fitted in the *Trento* and *Trieste*. These instruments actually did not succeed in giving any reading before opening fire,[18] and even afterwards their observations were 'jumpy', uncertain and inaccurate."

The sea was smooth and visibility good (15 miles). The enemy concentrated on the *Gloucester*, which zig-zagged to avoid being hit. At 0829 the range had decreased to 23,500 yards and the *Gloucester* fired three salvoes which, though falling short, caused the Italian cruisers to alter course away and draw outside the British gun range; there resuming a parallel course the Italian cruisers continued firing, though their salvoes were all falling short. Both forces continued speeding to the south-east when at 0854 the aspect of affairs was abruptly changed by a report of enemy battleships. This originated from British aircraft 5F which had seen at 0805 what appeared to be a force of three enemy battleships in a position 34° N., 24° 16' E., steering to the south-west (210°) at 20 knots. As Vice-Admiral Pridham-Wippell at 0805 had been only seven miles from that identical position and must have sighted them himself had they been there, he considered the position was "manifestly incorrect",[19] but there remained the possibility of enemy battleships being somewhere in the vicinity. At 0855 the enemy cruisers ceased fire, and turning to port went off to the north westward on an approximate course of 300°, having been ordered by the Italian C.-in-C. to break off the engagement, as he considered that his cruisers were being drawn too far into waters under control of our aviation. The VALF reported the enemy's alteration of course and decided to follow and try to maintain touch. At 0936 he reported the enemy still in sight bearing 320°, 16 miles, course 320° speed 28 knots. During this phase of the action the *Vendetta* developed engine trouble, and was detached to Alexandria.

Fig. 1

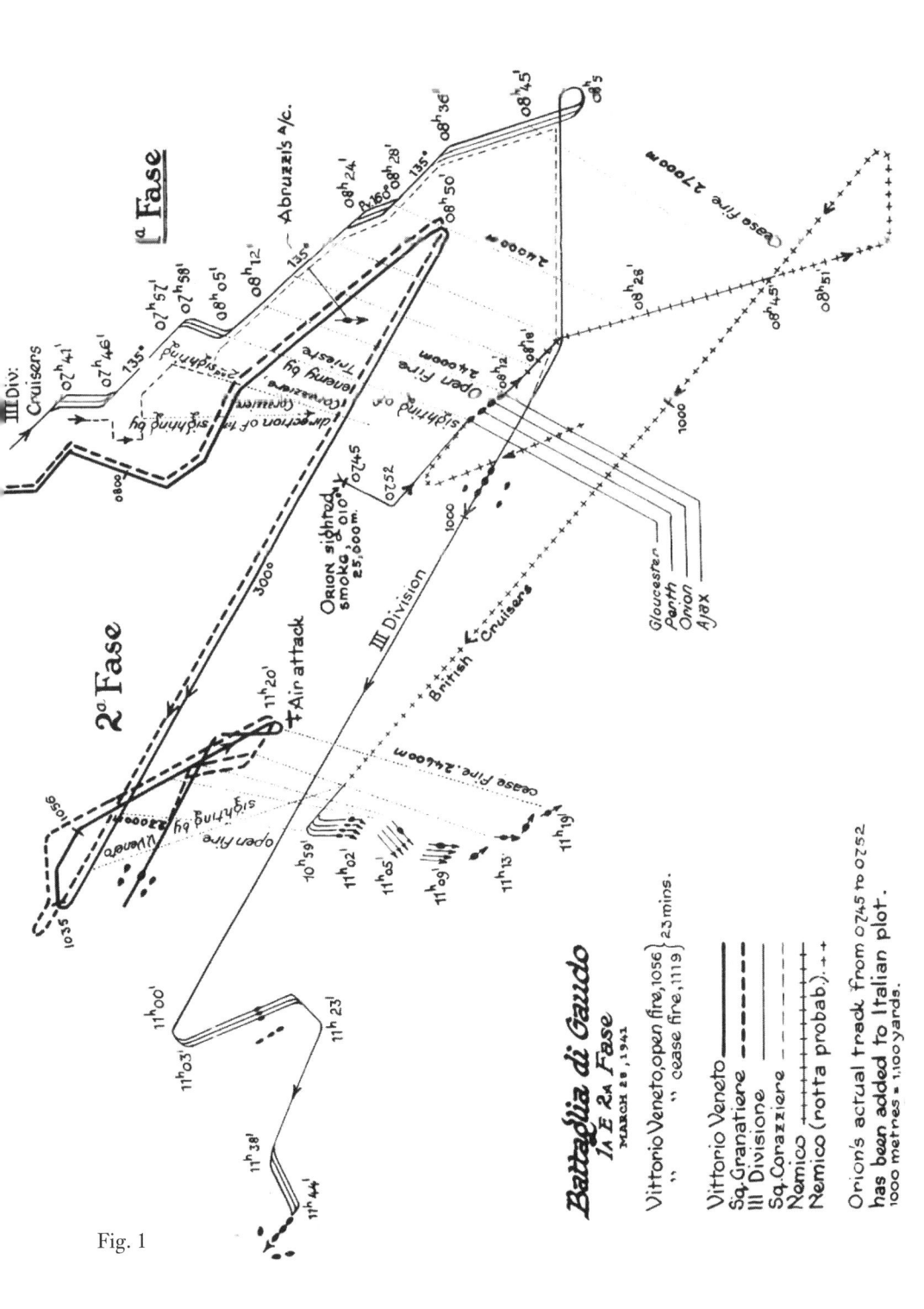

The C.-in-C.'s Movements, 28 March

Meanwhile the C.-in-C.,[20] after receiving at 0827 the Vice-Admiral's sighting report of 0802, had increased speed to 22 knots (0832) and altered course to 310°. The situation did not for the moment appear "unduly alarming", but twenty minutes later he ordered the *Valiant* (0851) to proceed at her utmost speed to join VALF, detaching the *Nubian* and *Mohawk* to accompany her. The *Warspite* (with slight condenser trouble)[21] and the *Barham* remained in company with the *Formidable* (Plan 1), which had been ordered at 0833 to range a torpedo striking force, while the aircraft at Maleme were also ordered at 0849[22] to attack the enemy cruisers (See page 46). Aircraft reports were then coming in indicating another enemy force to the northward, though their presence was by no means certain. Aircraft 5F's report (at 0805) of battleships might be correct, or on the other hand she might be mistaking cruisers for battleships, a not uncommon error at the time arising from the similar silhouettes of the *Cavour* class battleships and the cruiser *Garibaldi* class, two of which were with Force Z. At 0847 the C.-in-C. received a report from aircraft 5F that touch was lost with the enemy cruisers and destroyers (probably enemy Force X), which she had reported at 0839 well to the southward of the 0722 position given by aircraft 5B.

By 0918, the C.-in-C. knew that the enemy cruisers: (Force X) had broken off action and were retiring to the north-west, being reported by VALF and aircraft 5H as steering 320° or 300° respectively, speed 28 knots. At about this time the *Gloucester*'s aircraft, which had been catapulted for spotting duty at 0831, reported another enemy force[23] to the northward of Force X. This report was not received in any other ship as the aircraft did not use the correct frequency nor was it passed on by the *Gloucester*. The receipt of this signal in the flagship would have helped to dispel the uncertainty created by indefinite and confusing reports received from the reconnaissance aircraft, which were not using "Duty letters" and in some cases were omitting their position.

Plan 3

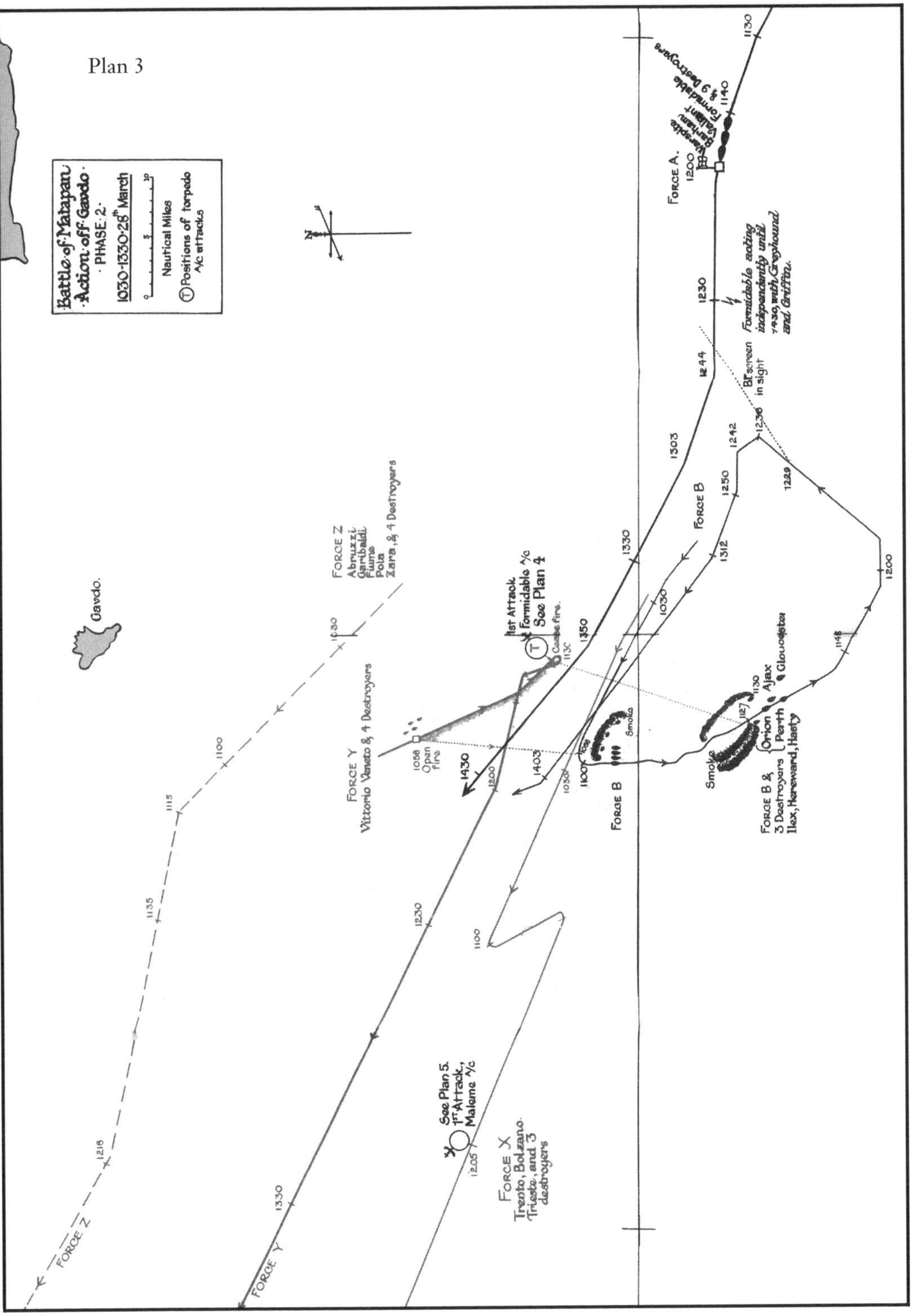

Battle of Matapan
Action off Gavdo
PHASE 2
1030-1330 28th March
Nautical Miles
Positions of torpedo A/c attacks
Gavdo.
Force Z
Abruzzi
Garibaldi
Fiume
Pola
Zara, & 4 Destroyers
Force Y
Vittorio Veneto & 4 Destroyers
Open fire
1st Attack
Formidable A/c
See Plan 4
Force A.
Warspite
Barham
Valiant
Formidable
& 9 Destroyers
Formidable acting independently until 1430, with Greyhound and Griffin.
Br screen in sight
Force B
Smoke
Orion
Ajax
Gloucester
Perth
Force B & 3 Destroyers
Ilex, Hereward, Hasty
See Plan 5.
1st Attack, Maleme A/c
Force X
Trento, Bolzano
Trieste, and 3 destroyers
Force Z
Force Y

At 0922, the C.-in-C. decided to hold back the *Formidable*'s striking force until the situation cleared and a signal was accordingly sent (0925) to R.A.F. 201 Group to send his flying boats to locate and shadow the enemy fleet in the Crete-Africa area between 25° and 23° E.

THE BATTLE OF MATAPAN

Plan 4

FIRST TORPEDO ATTACK 1127
BY
826 AND 829 SQUADRONS (FORMIDABLE).

HMS *Formidable*'s First Striking Force Takes Off

In order to relieve the pressure on our cruisers, at 0939 the C.-in-C. ordered the *Formidable* to fly off a torpedo striking force to attack cruisers in sight of VALF or other squadron of enemy cruisers if sighted. This order was carried out at 0956 by 5 Albacores (826 Sqdn.) and 1 Albacore (829 Sqdn.) with an escort of two Fulmars (803 Sqdn.). A Swordfish (826 Sqdn.) also took off for "Action Observation, Duty J". The striking force was armed with Mark 12 torpedoes with duplex pistols, set to 400 yards safety range, 40 knots speed and a depth setting of 34 ft. This setting the observers in three planes succeeding in altering to 28 feet when it was known that cruisers were the target of attack.

Meanwhile the *Orion* and cruisers of Force B were following hard (course 310°) in the wake of the enemy cruisers (Force X) which were barely in sight 16 miles away. A number of aircraft were sighted and Force B between 1045 and 1100 fired on several, including some of our own.

About 1045 the enemy was again visible from the *Orion*'s director, but nothing more had been heard of the three battleships reported by aircraft, '5F' to the northward and the VALF came to the conclusion that they were in reality his own cruisers.

Plan 5

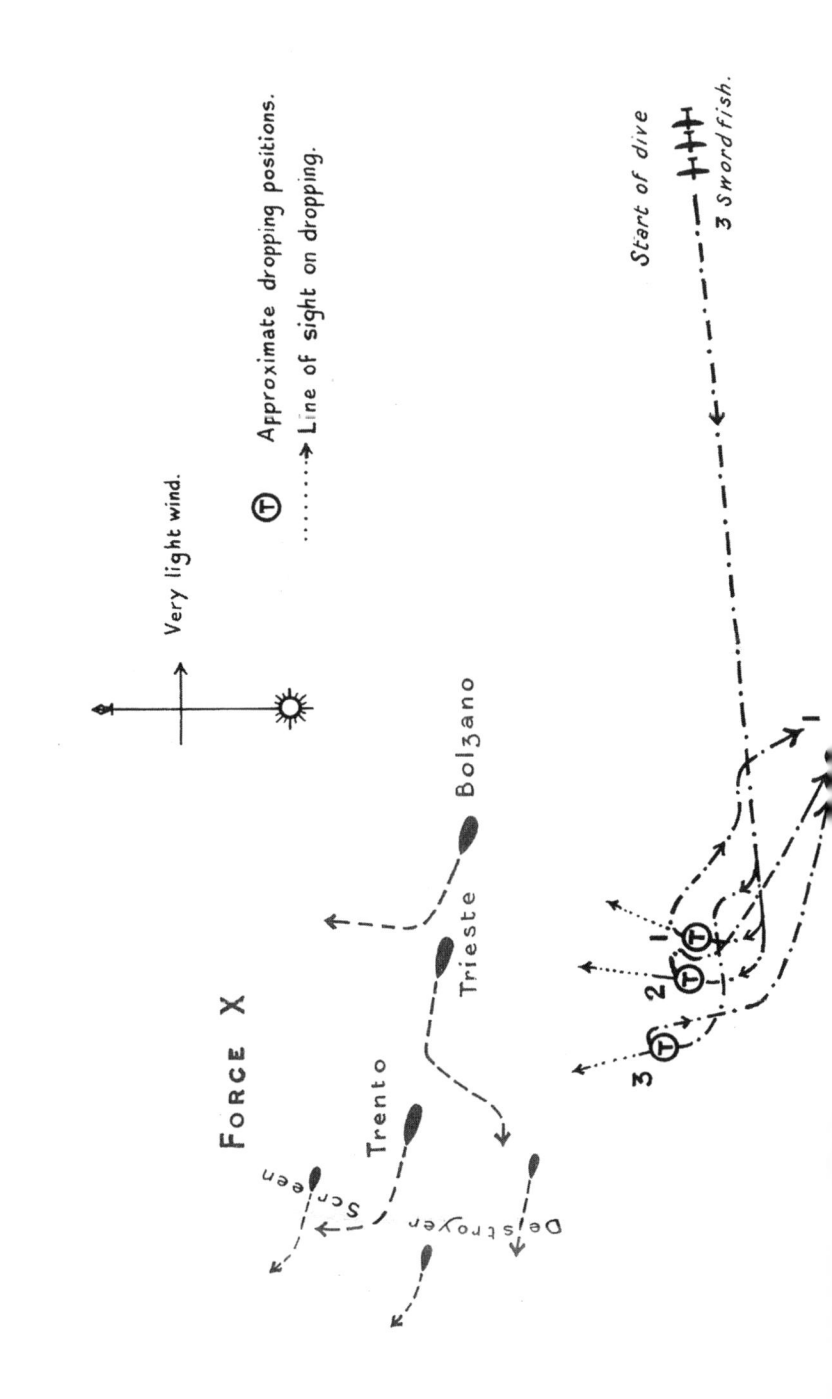

THE BATTLE OF MATAPAN

TORPEDO ATTACK, 1205
BY
815 SQUADRON (MALEME).

Action with the Italian Battleship

The enemy's motive in breaking off action and retiring to the north-west was revealed in dramatic fashion at 1058 when the *Orion* sighted an enemy battleship (later known to be the *Vittorio Veneto*), bearing 002° (Force Y in Plan 3). Her appearance "put a very different complexion on affairs". The enemy was fast and the *Gloucester*'s maximum safe speed was expected to be 24 knots. It looked as if the British cruisers might be "sandwiched" between the *Vittorio Veneto* to the north and the Italian cruisers (Force X) to the north-west (see Fig. 1). The battleship quickly opened fire and the VALF at once altered course together to the southward in order to disengage, increasing speed to 30 knots, a speed which fortunately the *Gloucester* successfully achieved. It was then 1059. For ten minutes the enemy concentrated on the *Orion* which suffered only minor damage from a near miss. The enemy's shooting at 32,000 yards was remarkably accurate; the *Veneto* fired 94 rounds in 29 salvoes out of which there were 11 mis-fires. Force B was ordered to make smoke, the wind at the time being about E.N.E., Force 2 and the smoke soon became effective, though the *Gloucester*, the only ship remaining visible to the enemy, was repeatedly straddled until the *Hasty* was able to reach a position where it was possible to cover her with smoke. The Italian battleship on the port quarter of our cruisers possessed an equal turn of speed, and at 1100 the 3rd Division of 8-in. cruisers reversed course to engage from the starboard quarter, a situation that might have become serious if the *Formidable*'s striking force had not at this critical moment opportunely intervened.

The First Attack on the *Vittorio Veneto*

Flying at 9,000 ft. the aircraft sighted the *Vittorio Veneto* at 1058 steering in a south-easterly direction[24] and shortly afterwards observed her salvoes straddling our cruisers. The planes proceeded to manoeuvre to reach a position off her starboard bow on the opposite side of the destroyer escort.

They attacked at 1127 in two waves, each plane being free to act independently (see Plan 4). The enemy destroyers began to move over to starboard as our aircraft commenced their dive, and the *Vittorio Veneto* altered course more than 180° to starboard when the first sub-flight was at 1,000 feet. Two aircraft (4A, 4F) already committed to the attack, released their torpedoes on her starboard side (bearing Green 70 and 50), the third (4C) attacking from fine on the starboard bow. The second sub-flight (5A, 4P, 4K) was able to take advantage of the *Vittorio Veneto*'s turn and dropped their torpedoes from good positions on her port bow. Although the striking force reported one probable hit, in fact all six tracks passed clear astern of the target.

Intense opposition, in the form of light and heavy A.A. fire and a splash barrage, was encountered by the attacking aircraft and during the approach two Junkers 88 attempted to intercept, one being shot down by the escorting Fulmars and the other driven off. From the viewpoint of removing the threat to our cruisers the attack had a fortunate and immediate result, for the *Vittorio Veneto*, breaking off her action with the British cruiser force, retired on a north-westerly course at a speed of 25 knots. From the Commander-in-Chief's viewpoint, however, the result was not altogether fortunate because his chances of bringing the enemy to action were considerably lessened.[25]

The VALF steering south all this time did not see the air attack and did not hear of it until a signal from the *Gloucester* got through the smoke at 1138. When the smoke screens cleared away and the horizon was at last clear, there was nothing in sight, and course was altered to make contact with the battle fleet. The enemy battleship seemed to have been previously steering a course approximately 160° at 31 knots and it was thought that the enemy cruisers (Force X) were probably closing in from the north-westward, though actually they had resumed a west-north-westerly course at high speed.

When touch was gained with the C.-in-C. about 1230,[26] the reference position of the Battle Fleet was found to differ by 10 miles from that of the Cruiser Squadron.

Attack by Maleme Striking Force on the 3rd Division

The aircraft from Maleme also took part in this phase of the action. Though the C.-in-C.'s signal (0849) to attack enemy cruisers in 33° 50' N., 24° 15' E., was not received at Maleme until 1005 a strenuous effort was made to comply. Three Swordfish which had just returned from dawn patrol were at once refuelled and flown off at 1050, armed with Mk. 12 torpedoes set to 20 feet. Flying at 9,000 feet they sighted at 1200 the enemy cruisers (Force X) in 34° 22' N., 23° 02' E.[27] steering 300° at 28 to 30 knots. They attacked from out of the sun at 1205 dropping their torpedoes at 1 to 2 miles on the enemy's port quarter (see Plan 5).

Their target was the rear cruiser (*Bolzano*). The two leading aircraft dropped their torpedoes on her port bow and beam. The third being at too great a height, turned to port and dropped his on the bow of the target. The enemy took avoiding action about five seconds after the first torpedoes were released, the leading and rear ships turning to starboard and the centre ship to port, and all the torpedoes missed. A.A. fire was opened when the aircraft were close to the water but none were damaged.

Movements of the British Battle Fleet (Force A)

It will be remembered that when the VALF first reported enemy cruisers in sight, the *Valiant* at 0851 had been ordered ahead of the battle fleet to support him. On hearing at 0918 that the enemy had broken off the action, the C.-in-C. cancelled the signal to *Valiant*[28] and ordered the *Nubian* and *Mohawk* to resume their screening positions. The only hope of delaying the enemy now lay in air attack and the C.-in-C. at 1112 asked R.A. (A) when the *Formidable*'s second striking force would be ready. R.A. (A) replied, "In about half an hour".

The VALF's signal of 1059 (received at 1107), reporting an enemy battleship, had however modified the situation and when the *Formidable* reported the 2nd striking force ready to fly off at 1153, the C.-in-C. told R.A. (A) to "hold it for the moment", as it might have an opportunity with the battle fleet in action, and at 1156 made a general signal – "Enemy battle fleet bears 290° distant 45 miles from me" (Plan 1). At 1225 the battle fleet was ordered to catapult their spotting aircraft in anticipation of a fleet action, each was given a specific duty and they were instructed to make for Suda Bay before exhausting their fuel. Course had been altered to 290° at 1135 and to 270° at 1200, then back to 290° at 1230, as the C.-in-C. at this stage still hoped to overtake the *Vittorio Veneto*, though he realised that the prospect of doing so depended on her speed being reduced by our air attacks.

Meanwhile the *Orion* and her cruisers had been retiring on the battle fleet, and at 1228 the *Orion* was sighted[29] by the *Jervis* bearing 210°. To the C.-in-C.'s signal – "When last did you see enemy", the VALF replied, "Enemy battle fleet last seen at 1116 bearing 312°, 26 miles from my present position on course 360°".[30] (T.O.O. 1245.) At 1305, the cruisers of Force B were ordered to proceed ahead of the battle fleet on a bearing of 290° at maximum visual signalling distance. They remained with the battle fleet until 1644 when they were ordered to press on and gain touch with the retreating enemy.

THE BATTLE OF MATAPAN

SECOND TORPEDO ATTACK, 1525, BY 829 SQUADRON (FORMIDABLE).

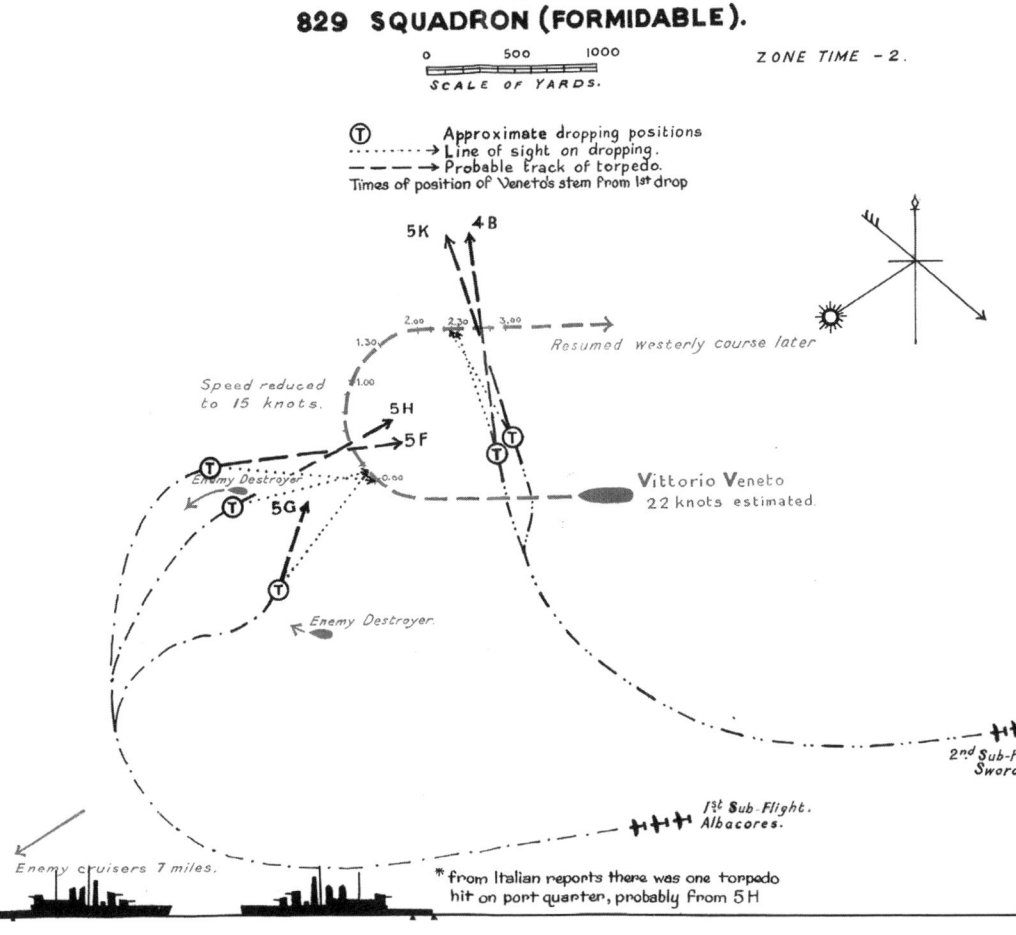

SCALE OF YARDS: 0 — 500 — 1000

ZONE TIME −2.

(T) Approximate dropping positions
······→ Line of sight on dropping.
– – –→ Probable track of torpedo.
Times of position of Veneto's stem from 1st drop

5K 4B

2.00 2.30 3.00
1.30
Speed reduced to 15 knots. 1.00
5H
5F
Enemy Destroyer
0.00
5G

Resumed westerly course later

Vittorio Veneto
22 knots estimated.

Enemy Destroyer.

2nd Sub-Flight Swordfish

1st Sub-Flight. Albacores.

Enemy cruisers 7 miles.

*from Italian reports there was one torpedo hit on port quarter, probably from 5H

Plan 6

The *Formidable's* Second Striking Force Awaits Orders

The *Formidable*'s first striking force returned between 1200 and 1215 after attacking the *Vittorio Veneto*. This necessitated flying off the second flight in order to allow the first to land on. The two operations were completed by 1244 and the *Formidable* proceeded to rejoin the battle fleet. The second striking force, consisting of three Albacores and two Swordfish (829 Sqdn.) accompanied by two escorting Fulmars (803 Sqdn.) was armed with Mark 12 torpedoes, set to 34 feet with duplex pistols and was ordered to wait overhead until the battle fleet engaged or attacked at 1330.

Whilst proceeding to rejoin the C.-in-C. the *Formidable* was attacked by two torpedo aircraft (S. 79s). The fighter patrol could do nothing as the enemy aircraft were only sighted a few minutes before delivering their attack. Their torpedoes were released at over 2,000 yards, one fine on the port bow and the other on the starboard bow. It was fortunately not difficult to comb their tracks, which passed astern. At 1400 the *Formidable* rejoined the flag ship[31] and the C.-in-C., with his whole fleet concentrated, continued the chase to the westward in pursuit of the enemy.

Position at 1330

At 1330 the enemy appeared to be in two groups – a southern and a northern; the southern group apparently consisted of one battleship (a *Vittorio*),[32] three cruisers and seven destroyers, last seen at 1130, 16 miles W.N.W. of VALF (steering to northward; the northern group apparently of two battleships, (*Cavour*),[33] three cruisers (two *Zara* and one *Pola*), and some destroyers last seen at 1200, west of Gavdo steering to westward.[34] This appreciation, based on the conflicting evidence available at the time, was issued in a signal at 1400. Later it was considered that the Italian forces were actually in three distinct groups[35] as follows (see Plan 1):–

(1) Force X, the 3rd Cruiser Division, consisting of three cruisers (the *Trento, Trieste* and *Bolzano*) and three destroyers, bore about 291° some 100 miles from the *Warspite* and some 37 miles west of the *Vittorio Veneto* (Y).
(2) Force Y, the battleship *Vittorio Veneto* and four destroyers some 65 miles 297° from the *Warspite*.
(3) Force Z, five cruisers; viz., three 8-in., 1st Division (*Zara, Fiume, Pola*): and two 6-in., 8th Division (*Giuseppe Garibaldi. Duca Degli Abruzzi*), with six destroyers. This force bore approximately 315° 95 miles from the *Warspite*.

The whole Italian force of one battleship, eight cruisers and 13 destroyers was making as hard as it could to the westward with Admiral Cunningham and the British fleet in hot pursuit. In the afternoon the wind dropped altogether, enabling the Battle Fleet to keep a steady 20 knots and not having to wait for flying operations. Had the strong north-easterly wind of the forenoon continued the C.-in-C. considered that the action might never have come off.

The Second Attack on the *Vittorio Veneto*
(Plan 6)

The wind had veered and lessened and the *Formidable* proceeding at full speed was able to land and fly off aircraft while still maintaining her station. As touch with the enemy had been lost owing to shortage of shadowing aircraft,[36] three Albacores, which had returned with the first striking force, were sent off again at 1400. One of them (4F) sighted the *Vittorio* at 1459, reporting her at 1515 in 34° 45' N., 22° 14' E. and continued to shadow her right up to the arrival of a relief at 1920. The second striking force sighted her at 1510 in 34° 50' N., 22° 10' E., screened by two destroyers on either bow. The squadron leader (Lieut.-Commander J. Dalyell Stead) worked up into the sun and succeeded in getting down to 5,000 feet unobserved. The leading destroyer on the battleship's port bow then opened fire but turned away when shot up by the fighter escort. As the three Albacores (5F, 5G, 5H) attacked on the *Vittorio*'s port bow she turned 180° to starboard and splashes were seen on her port bow and amidships. Two Swordfish (4B, 5K) had worked round "up sun" to attack separately; but as the *Vittorio* in turning presented her starboard side clear of the screen, they decided to attack together and dived from 8,000 feet. The *Vittorio* had turned by that time (1525) and was making 14 knots, thus providing an easy shot. A large splash was seen on her starboard quarter and another on her starboard side. Of the five torpedoes launched only one gained a hit,[37] which caused a reduction in the *Vittorio Veneto*'s speed. A description of the final movements of the squadron leader (Lieut.-Commander J. Dalyell-Stead), who obtained the hit and was unfortunately lost, is given in Admiral Iachino's book, (see Appendix G). The Italian C.-in-C. refers to a bombing attack immediately following the 3-Albacore torpedo attack, but does not mention the 2-Swordfish torpedo attack.

RAF Bombers from Greece

During the afternoon of 28 March R.A.F. bombers from Greece, in accordance with arrangements made the day before, made a series of attacks on the *Veneto* and both cruiser divisions. At Menidi airfield (near Tatoi some 20 miles north of Athens) 24 Blenheims[38] were being held in readiness and 6 at Paramythia (in Janina, the province opposite Corfu).

When an enemy battleship report was received from an R.A.F. Sunderland at 1235/28 March six aircraft of 84 Squadron were ordered from Menidi to find and attack it. Her position at 1330 was estimated to be 35° 11' N., 22° 15' E.[39] This position was on the track of the *Zara* group, that is the First Division of Cruisers (called in British reports Force Z) but rather ahead of them. The attack was made at 1420 in an estimated position of 35° 10' N., 22° 10' E.[40] but was probably on the *Veneto* and not Force Z, since no report of an attack on Force Z at this time is mentioned by Admiral Iachino; though he does report the *Veneto* being attacked unsuccessfully by bombers at 1420 and 1450. The 3rd Division (*Trieste*) was attacked at 1520 and two hits were claimed on one cruiser with 250 lb bombs and two on another with 500 lb. bombs; unfortunately these were only "near misses" on the *Trento* and *Bolzano*. Several attacks were made on Force Z between 1515 and 1645, when "near misses" were obtained on the *Zara*[41] and the *Garibaldi*. This was the first instance in the Mediterranean of land-based bombers taking part in active operations with the Fleet against enemy Fleet at sea.

The following tabular statement showing the total number of our aircraft attacks on enemy ships during 28 March, has been compiled after studying both R.A.F., F.A.A. and Italian reports:–

The allocation of attacks (right) of particular R.A.F. Squadrons to specified targets is probably correct, but cannot be proved exactly.

Time	Position	Type of Aircraft		Target	Weapon	Result
		No.	Squadron			
1120 to 1130	34° 06' N. 23° 58' E.	6 Albacores 2 Fulmars	F.A.A. (*Formidable*) 826 803	*V. Veneto*	Torpedo 6	No hits
1205	34° 04' N. 23° 22' E.	3 Swordfish	F.A.A. (Maleme) 815	3rd Division (*Trieste*) Force X	Torpedo 3	No hits
1420	34° 38' N. 22° 30' E.	3 Blenheims	R.A.F. 84	*V. Veneto* Force Y	Bombs	No hits
1450	34° 42' N. 22° 15' E.	6 Blenheims	113	*V. Veneto* Force Y	Bombs	No hits
1510 to 1525	34° 50' N. 22° 00' E.	3 Albacores 2 Swordfish 2 Fulmars	F.A.A. (*Formidable*) 829 803	*V. Veneto* Force Y	Torpedo 5 and bombs	1 hit by torpedo
1520 1700	34° 49' N. 21° 50' E. 35° 03' N. 21° 21' E.	4 Blenheims 6 Blenheims	R.A.F. 84 211	3rd Division (*Trieste*) Force X	Bombs	"Near Misses" on *Trento* and *Bolzano*
1515 to 1645	Between 35° 30' N. 21° 22' E. and 35° 43' N. 20° 58' E.	6 Blenheims 5 Blenheims	R.A.F. 113 84	1st Division (*Zara*) Force Z	Bombs Bombs	"Near Misses" on *Zara* and *Garibaldi*
1930 to 1950	35° 15' N. 20° 58' E	6 Albacores 4 Swordfish	F.A.A. 826 (*Formidable*) (2) 829 (*Formidable*) (2) 815 (Maleme)	1st Division (*Zara*)	Torpedo 10	*Pola* 1 hit

BATTLE OF MATAPAN
TORPEDO ATTACKS AT DUSK (1930-1950)
BY
826 SQUADRON (FORMIDABLE)
AND 815 SQUADRON (MALEME)
Positions of aircraft & forces of Italian Fleet are approx.

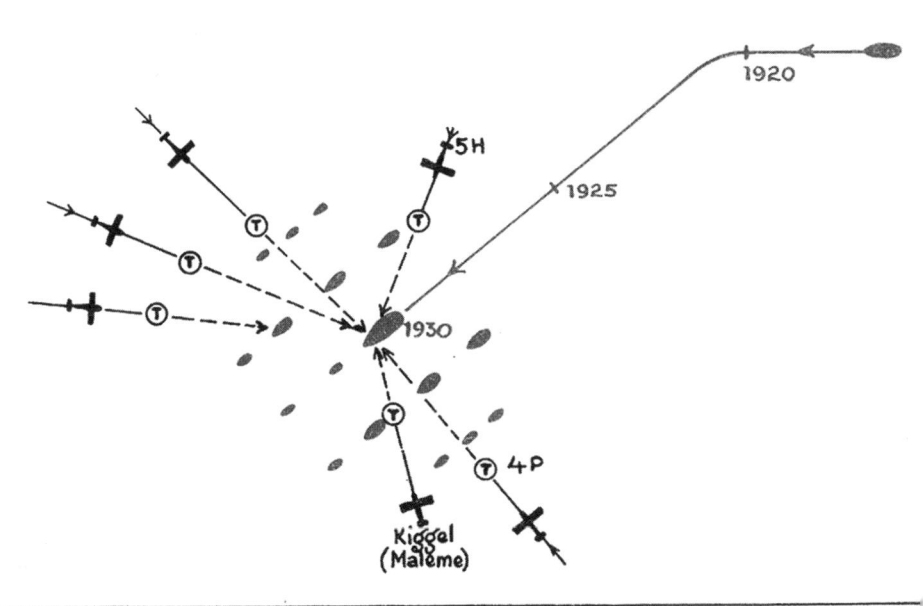

ATTACK BY LT TORRENS SPENCE
815 SQUADRON (MALEME)

ATTACK BY AIRCRAFT 5A
SUB-LT(A) G.P.C. WILLIAMS

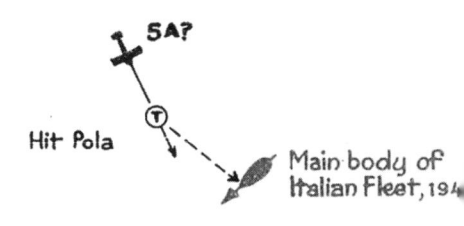

Plan 7

The Pursuit 1330 – 1810

The Fleet Air Arm at Maleme (in Crete) was equally intent on its task. As soon as the first striking force returned at 1330, preparations were begun to send out another. Lieutenant Torrens-Spence (C.O. 815 Squadron) arrived from Eleusis with the only serviceable Swordfish and the only torpedo left on the mainland of Greece, and Maleme was able to muster two more. Communications at Maleme were extremely difficult as signals were coming in by roundabout routes and were subjected to long delay.[42] As the "Pack" Set at that station could not receive wireless messages from Suda Bay, a Fulmar was sent off to check the enemy's position and course and to return at once with the information. It returned at 1600 with the information required.

Admiral Cunningham's target was the damaged battleship, but the situation was obscure and conflicting air reports did little to clear it up. At 1600 the C.-in-C. ordered the *Formidable* to make as strong a T/B attack as possible on the single battleship at dusk.[43] At 1618 the destroyers were ordered to be organized in divisions for the night attack and at 1644 VALF was directed to press on and gain touch with the damaged battleship estimated then to bear 282° 58 miles. Five minutes later (1649) came in a signal from the Rear-Admiral (A) in the *Formidable* reporting three possible hits in the attack at 1510 and the C.-in-C. replied "well done".

This was good news and opened up a prospect of further success, for one of her aircraft had already reported at 1558 (received at 1607) a large decrease in the battleship's speed, which tended to corroborate the R.A.'s report and gave hopes of her being closer than expected. Vice-Admiral Pridham-Wippell's cruisers going 30 knots were pressing on ahead and at 1646 the destroyers *Nubian* and *Mohawk* were ordered to proceed ahead of the Battle Fleet and act as a visual link between the Battle Fleet and the cruisers.[44] Evening was beginning to fall and the destroyers at 1720 were organized for a night attack.[45]

To the C.-in-C. the situation up to 1800 was far from clear. "This was due to the presence of both ship-borne and shore-based reconnaissance aircraft, a considerable change of wind, the presence of several separate enemy squadrons and finally the ever present difficulty of distinguishing the silhouette of enemy warships."[46]

At 1810 the C.-in-C. signalled his intentions to the fleet. "If cruisers gain touch with damaged battleship, 2nd and 14th Destroyer Flotillas will be sent to attack. If she is not then destroyed, battle fleet will follow in. If not located by cruisers I intend to work round to the north and then west and regain touch in the morning." The *Mohawk* and *Nubian* were ordered to join the 14th Destroyer Flotilla at dusk. The 2nd and 14th Destroyer Flotillas were to form 45°, one mile on either bow; the 10th Flotilla to take station ahead.

Towards evening the situation became clearer. At 1745 *Warspite*'s aircraft, purposely held for this particular purpose, had been catapulted for the second time with an experienced observer (Lieut.-Commander A.S. Bolt, D.S.C.). He sighted the *Vittorio Veneto* at 1820 and "at 1831 made the first of a series of reports which rapidly cleared up the situation". By 1832 it was evident that the damaged Italian battleship accompanied by three cruisers and seven destroyers was some 50 miles 292° from the C.-in-C., and was apparently steering about 300° at 12 knots. At 1846 the C.-in-C. ordered the battleships to assume the third organisation[47] and at 1849 formed single line ahead and increased speed to 20 knots. At 1855 Lieut.-Commander Bolt reported the enemy forces to be concentrating and at 1912 to have formed in five columns.[48] As the light failed he closed in and took up a position four miles astern of the enemy at 2,000 feet where later on he had a good view of the dusk torpedo attack.[49]

His last report however presented the C.-in-C. with a difficult problem. "The enemy had concentrated in a mass which presented a most formidable obstacle to attack by cruisers and destroyers." By morning he would be drawing under cover of bombing aircraft from Sicily. The question was whether to send the destroyers in now to attack this difficult target or to wait until morning in the hope of engaging at dawn, but with the certainty of exposing the fleet to a heavy scale of air attack. This was not an attractive prospect, for the Commander-in-Chief was obliged to consider the eventuality of having to evacuate the army from Greece, for which he would need a strong supporting force to engage the enemy battle fleet if it risked an appearance. It was decided to attack at night with the destroyers and to follow up with the battle fleet.[50]

The Situation at 1915, 28 March

The sun had set at 1840. By 1915 it appeared that the damaged enemy battleship was about 45 miles to the westward steering 290° at 15 knots.[51] Another cruiser force had joined the enemy fleet which was formed in five columns. The battleship was apparently in the centre with four destroyers screening ahead and two astern; on her port side were three 8-in. cruisers and outside them three destroyers; on her starboard side were three 8-in. cruisers with what appeared to be two 6-in. cruisers[52] on the starboard wing. The two *Garibaldi*'s[53] in Force Z (sometimes referred to in A/C reports as two battleships) had gone on to the westward. The three *Zara*'s had joined the *Vittorio Veneto*. At 1925, just before the *Formidable*'s dusk attack, the enemy's formation[54] as given above was confirmed by Duty A/C "Q". This was the disposition of the Italian fleet when the *Formidable*'s aircraft came bearing down on it.

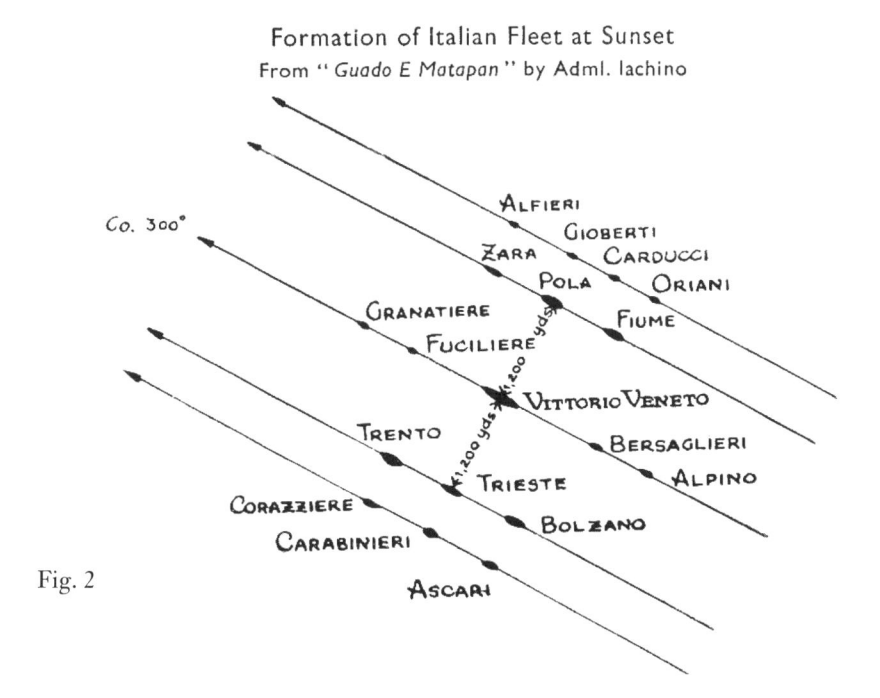

Fig. 2 — Formation of Italian Fleet at Sunset
From "*Guado E Matapan*" by Adml. Iachino

G.2331

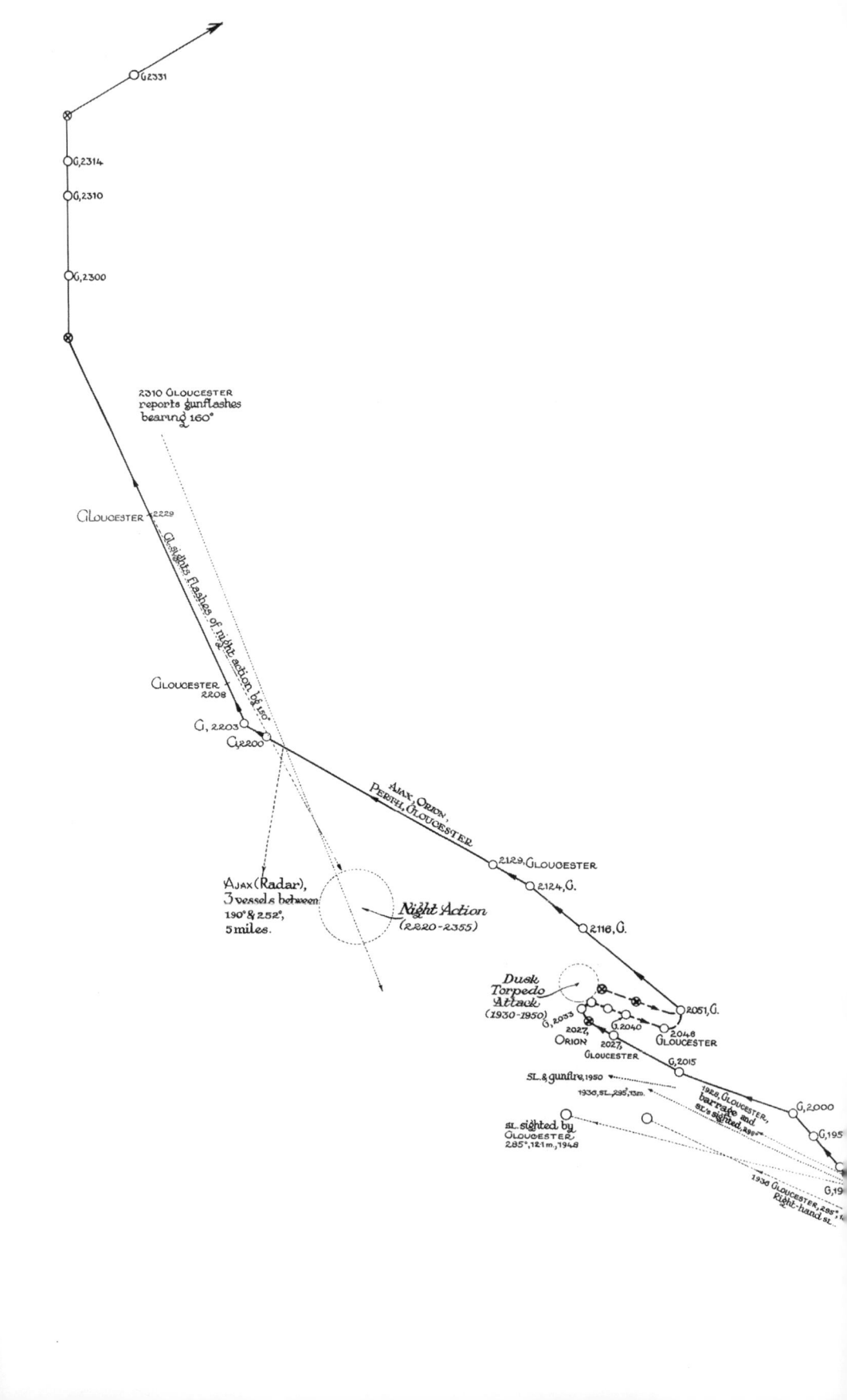

G.2314
G.2310

G.2300

2310 Gloucester
reports gunflashes
bearing 160°

Gloucester 2229

G. sights flashes of night action b. 150°

Gloucester 2208

G. 2203
G.2200

AJAX, ORION,
PERTH, GLOUCESTER

2129, GLOUCESTER
2124, G.

AJAX (Radar),
3 vessels between
190° & 252°,
5 miles.

Night Action
(2220-2355)

2118, G.

Dusk
Torpedo
Attack
(1930-1950)

2051, G.
G. 2053
2027,   G. 2040   2048
ORION   2027,   GLOUCESTER
         GLOUCESTER
                              G. 2015
S.L. & gunfire, 1950
1930, S.L., 285°, 13m.   1925, GLOUCESTER,
                            barrage and
                            a/c sighted, 285°   G.2000

S.L. sighted by   G.195
GLOUCESTER
285°, 12.1m., 1948
                                          1936 GLOUCESTER, 285°
                                          Right-hand S.L.   G.19

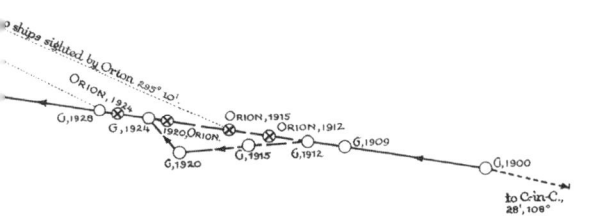

Plan 10

Third Torpedo Attack on the *Vittorio Veneto*

It was 1925 when the *Formidable* made her third and last attack. At 1735 in 34° 42' N., 22° 44' E., she flew off her third striking force of six Albacores of 826 Squadron and two Swordfish of 829 Squadron under the command of Lieut.-Commander W. H. G. Saunt. The sun was sinking when the force sighted the enemy and took up a waiting position astern and well out of range at a low height. It was joined by two aircraft from Maleme. In that distant airfield in Crete, with strenuous and enthusiastic effort a second striking force had been launched, consisting of two Swordfish, armed with torpedoes, piloted by Lieutenant F. M. A. Torrens-Spence and Lieutenant (A) L. J. Kiggell. They had sighted part of the enemy at 1810, 25 miles off, and on closing identified them as four ships screened by six destroyers, steering about 320° at about 14 knots. At 1835 they saw the *Formidable*'s force coming up from the eastward and took station in its rear. Dusk had fallen at 1925 when the *Formidable*'s aircraft swept in to attack. Duty A/C "Q" reported the enemy steering 230° during the approach, and as the eight aircraft closed to about 3,000 yards a tremendous barrage of flaming onions[55] and shell from A.A. and other guns rent the air over a wide arc. The aircraft were forced to turn away to starboard and losing their formation had to attack independently from very different angles. Most of the pilots thought they had fired at the *Vittorio Veneto*, but in the heavy barrage with searchlights flashing in every direction it was extremely difficult to observe anything with precision. Several observers, however, reported a hit on a cruiser, which in the light of subsequent reports proved to have been the *Pola*. Aircraft 5A (Sub-Lieutenant (A) C. P. C. Williams) was the last to attack at 1945 and as the *Pola* was torpedoed at 1946 it was probably his torpedo that hit her.[56] He was seen by the Italians flying just above the water pressing in to short range under a withering fire.

The two Maleme craft made their attack separately. Lieutenant Torrens-Spence saw the Italian ships shrouded in piebald smoke screens, black and white. The dazzling glare of the searchlights, the flaring tracers and the flash of guns greatly impeded accurate observation. Climbing to get a better view, he glided down to the starboard bow of a cruiser towards the rear of the starboard column and dropped his torpedo at 1950 at a range of about 450 yards. His aircraft was hit but he made a successful get-away and landed at Maleme at 2120. Lieutenant Kiggell in the second Maleme craft, seeing the *Formidable*'s Albacores attack on the enemy's starboard side, decided to attack from port. Closing in slowly to the edge of the smoke screen he fired at 900-1,000 yards, some 100 yards ahead of the smoke. As he turned away, a large ship and a destroyer could be seen emerging from the smoke screen.

The *Formidable*'s aircraft having completed their attack made for Suda Bay, which they reached between 2100 and 2300. Aircraft 5A, short of petrol, made a forced landing near the destroyer *Juno* which rescued the crew.

The attack had important results. The *Pola* was hit on the starboard side between the engine and boiler room, causing her main engines to stop and putting out of action all her electrical power, and with it all her turrets. The attack was observed by the *Formidable*'s night shadower which had relieved *Warspite*'s Duty "Q". The shadower reported at 1950 that the enemy force had divided, the major portion going off on a course 220° while the "battleship" remained stopped with smoke rising from her. This report was never received,[57] which was just as well in view of the fact that the course steered by the whole force from 1930 was 300° and not 220°.

Movements of the British Battle Fleet

By 1920 the C.-in-C. was aware of the position and formation of the enemy fleet and knew that Vice-Admiral Pridham-Wippell with the cruisers in Force B was in touch with it.[58]

The report[59] of the dusk attack received at 2008 mentioned only probable hits. It was in the light of this information that the C.-in-C. had to consider whether he would be justified in taking the fleet at night through a screening force of at least six cruisers and eleven destroyers with another force of what was reported as two battleships, three cruisers and five destroyers in the vicinity. On the other hand, if the enemy ships (who were only 320 miles from their base) could continue at 14 or 15 knots during the night they would be well under cover of German dive bombers at daylight, and the British fleet, even if it were able to intercept them at dawn, would almost certainly be subjected to a very heavy scale of air attack throughout the day. The C.-in-C. decided to accept a night action and at 2040 ordered the destroyers to attack.[60] Captain Mack with his eight destroyers going 28 knots drew ahead and made off with the intention of passing up the starboard side of the *Veneto*, out of visibility range and attacking from ahead.

VALF and the Cruisers of Force B
(Plan 10)

Meanwhile the VALF with the cruisers of Force B had been pressing on at 30 knots to the westward to get in touch (See pages 55-57) and at 1832 had seen the *Formidable*'s aircraft going up to attack. The Vice-Admiral, having decided to have his ships spread by 2000, ordered them at 1907 to spread on a line of bearing 020°, 7 miles apart. They were still opening out when at 1914 three or four enemy ships[61] were sighted on the starboard bow and the Vice-Admiral, deciding accordingly to keep his ships concentrated, ordered them to reform in line ahead. By 1930 the *Formidable*'s dusk torpedo attack had begun and was clearly visible below the horizon bearing about 303°, more or less ahead, some fifteen miles away. The enemy searchlights could be seen slanting through the smoke and the tracer shell of various colours soaring into the sky. "They must have been very gallant men who went through it" the VALF remarked in his report. At 1932, course was altered to 320° and as the enemy evidently had a large force in close formation, the Vice-Admiral decided to continue to keep his force concentrated, and at 1949 reduced his speed to 20 knots in order "to reduce bow waves".[62] The last stage of the air attack was still in progress. Searchlights and gunfire were visible bearing 278° and at 1950 course was altered to 290° towards them. Visibility to the westward was then about four miles, but there were no ships in sight. At 2014 the *Orion* altered course to 310° and a minute later a vessel was plotted by A.S.V. six miles ahead. Speed was reduced to 15 knots (2017) and over a period of eighteen minutes ranges were plotted proving that the vessel was stopped or moving very slowly.[63] The *Ajax* at 2029 sent out a report of an enemy ship in 35° 16' N., 21° 4' E. (275°, 5 miles from *Ajax*).

The ship was evidently "fixed" and the Vice-Admiral, Light Forces, decided to lead clear of her to the northward and regain touch with the remaining ships of the enemy.[64] Accordingly at 2033 he turned to 60° and at 2036 to 110°[65] together, reporting the enemy at 2040 to the C.-in-C.[66] Supposing that the 14th D.F. would proceed to attack the enemy in that position, VALF turned at 2048 to the north-westward (310°) to "continue in search of the remaining ships" altering at 2115 to 300° and going on at 2119 to 20 knots.

The cruisers had been proceeding for some time on this course and VALF was "considering spreading" them again "to find the remainder" of the Italian fleet when he realized that if Captain (D) went further west on the assumption that the enemy was moving at 13 knots "he would almost certainly encounter our cruisers". At 2155 the *Ajax* reported three unknown vessels by Radar 5 miles to the southward.[67] Though rather far to the westward these were thought to be our own flotillas "going up to attack"[68] and VALF decided to keep concentrated and "steer more to the North so as to keep clear of them". Accordingly at 2202 he turned to the northward to 340°, intending later to alter course and increase speed so as to intercept any of the enemy that might be on their way to Messina. As the enemy had been reported to have altered course to 230° during the dusk torpedo attack it seemed probable that he would be steering to the northward of 295° if, as the VALF thought, he was making for Messina.

At 2229 the flashes of the great guns of the battle fleet could be seen bearing astern 150° to 160°. Then at 2243 a "red light"[69] was sighted by the *Orion* and *Gloucester* bearing 320° on the port bow. The general alarm was made; the cruisers formed a single line ahead and course was altered to 000° at 2255.[70]

At 2314 a heavy explosion bearing 150° to 160° lit up the horizon away to the southward.[71] Shortly afterwards VALF received the C.-in-C.'s signal of 2312 ordering all forces not actually engaged to withdraw to the north, and at 2332 altered course to 60°. At 0018 the *Gloucester* sighted some "object" to the south-west, losing sight of it at 0030. This was unconfirmed by any other ship. Nothing more was seen until 0635 when the smoke of the battle fleet was sighted to the eastward.

Destroyer Striking Force
(Plan 1)

The *Ajax*'s report of the enemy was made at 2029 (See pages 63-64) and at 2037 the C.-in-C. ordered eight of the destroyers[72] that were with him to attack the enemy battle fleet, which was estimated at 2030 to bear from the Admiral 286°, 33 miles and to be steering 295°, 13 knots.[73] The destroyers increased to 28 knots at 2043 and drew ahead, still steering 300°. The 14th D.F. was in line ahead, with the 2nd D.F. six cables on its starboard beam. It was Captain Mack's intention to pass up the starboard side[74] of the damaged battleship out of visible range and attack her from ahead. At 2115 he informed the 2nd Flotilla and the Vice-Admiral of this intention and that he was going to alter course to 285° at 2200. He had not received the *Ajax*'s signal of 2029 reporting an enemy ship in 35° 16' N., 21° 04' E., nor the *Orion*'s signal of 2040 reporting a "stopped ship"[75] in 35° 18' N., 21° E.

This decision to go to the northward of the enemy battleship was considered "most unfortunate" by the C.-in-C. "as it cramped the cruiser squadron and left the southern flank of the enemy open for escape."[76] The enemy were reported turning to the S.W. at 1915 and steering 295° at the time D.14 was detached by the C.-in-C., but their turn to 323° at 2048 was not known at the time.[77]

At 2200 the cruisers on Captain (D)'s plot had drawn across to his starboard bow. It was just at this time that he received the *Ajax*'s report (of 2155) of three unknown ships which when plotted appeared to be four miles directly ahead of him[78] and were assumed by Captain (D) to refer to his own force though they were subsequently considered to be the *Zara* and *Fiume* (some 10 miles to the south-westward) on their way back to help the *Pola*.

As the destroyers proceeded to the westward the flash of the battleships' guns could be seen at 2230 on the port quarter. Ten minutes later (2240) the *Hasty* sighted a red light bearing 010°,[79] evidently the same as that which was seen to the north-westward by the *Orion* and *Gloucester* at the same time.

There seems little doubt that this was the remainder of the enemy fleet, or some portion of it, retiring to the north-west,[80] which by that time had

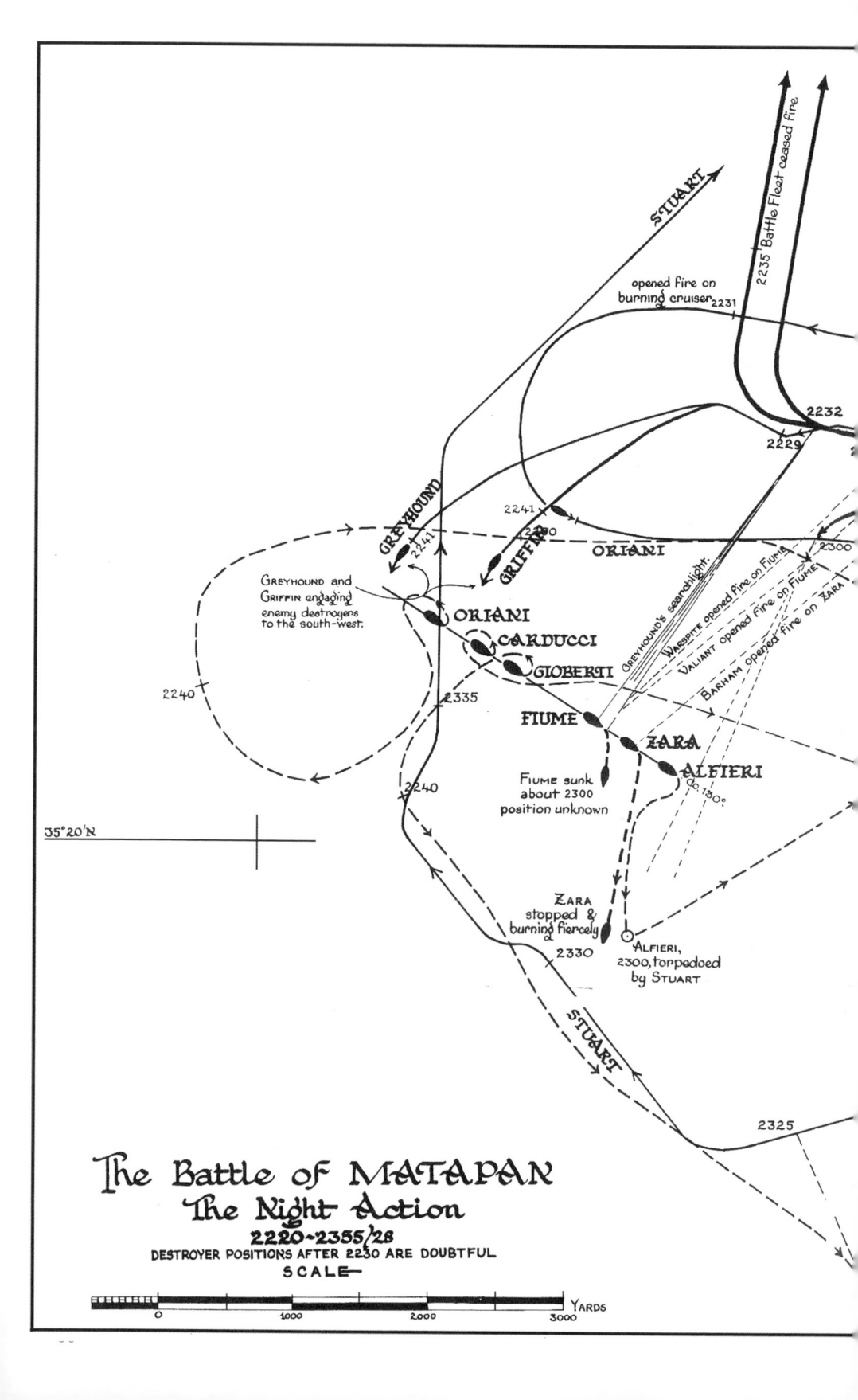

The Battle of MATAPAN
The Night Action
2220-2355/28
DESTROYER POSITIONS AFTER 2230 ARE DOUBTFUL

FORMIDABLE
STUART
2225
HAVOCK

WARSPITE
VALIANT
FORMIDABLE
BARHAM

GRIFFIN 2225
GREYHOUND 2226

Line of bearing, 100°

Stuart fired 8 torpedoes at Zara & dr. and opened fire on Zara

2305, opened fire on cruiser
STUART

2308

2310

my destroyer (RDUCCI) torpedoed d sunk by Havock at 2315.

2317, Stuart fired a few salvoes at ZARA

Havock fired 4 torpedoes 2315 at destroyer

HAVOCK

2345 Havock opened fire at Pola
2340

yer opped, urning. 315.

Undamaged enemy destroyer (Oriani) sighted by Stuart steaming past..

2330
2335

ORIANI and IOBERTI escaped.

Heavy gunfire heard by Havock about 2315

h small fire
y Stuart, 2325.

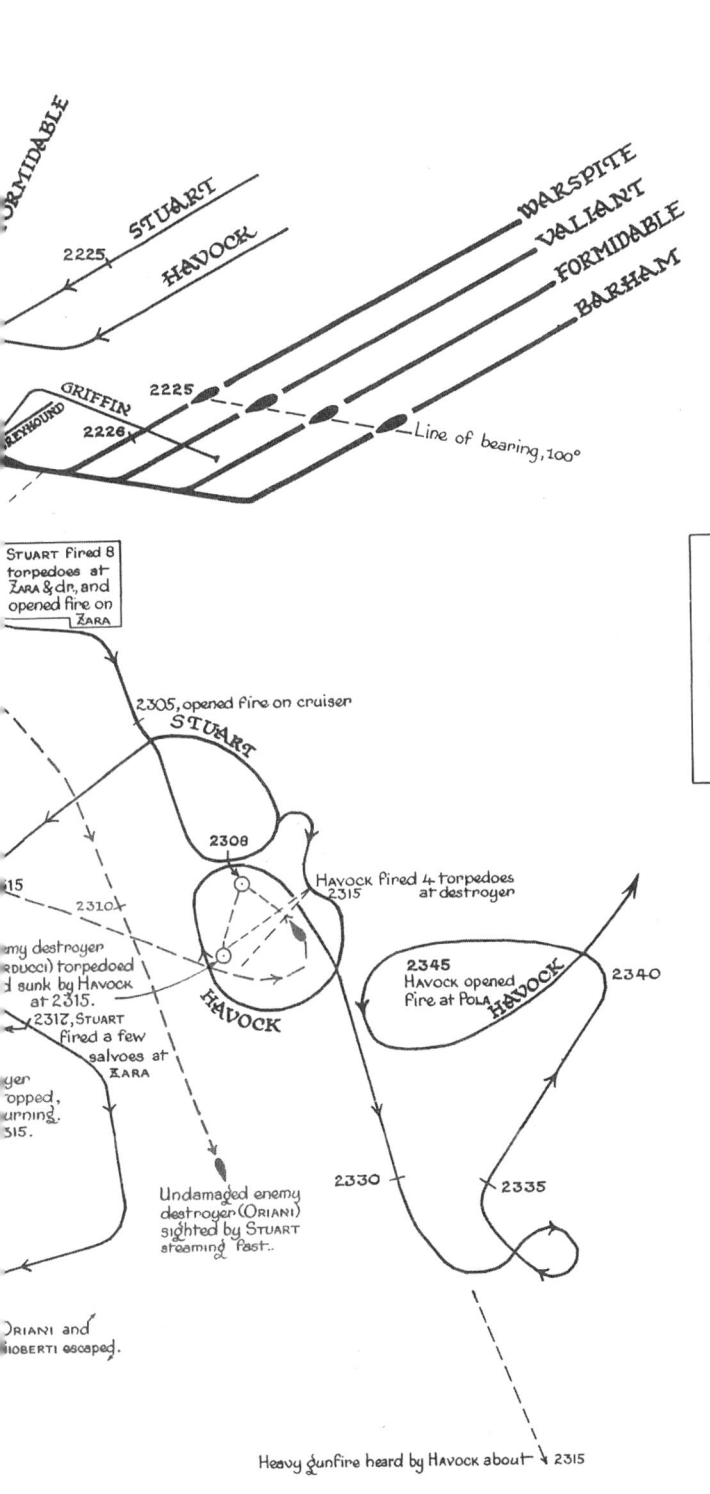

Torpedo Firing by destroyers:
STUART:- 8 torpedoes at Zara & dr. Hit on dr. (2300)
HAVOCK:- 4 torpedoes at dr. 2315, 1 hit.
4 torpedoes at Zara 2330, missed.

Plan 8

reached a position well to the northward of the destroyers and not very far from the cruisers.

The destroyers held on to the westward on the same course (285°), apparently assuming that the Italian fleet was steering to the westward on the course 295°, given in the C.-in-C.'s signal of 2037. At 2320 came a signal from the C.-in-C. to forces not engaged in sinking the enemy to retire to the north-east.[81] Captain (D) turning to the north-east asked at 2322 if the signal included his flotilla and was told "after your attack".[82] Receiving this reply at 2337 he turned again at 2340 to the westward, continuing on course 270° for twenty minutes. At midnight considering that he had drawn sufficiently ahead of the enemy to cross his track, Captain (D) altered to 200° and reduced to 20 knots. At 0030, just as he reached a position which he estimated to be right ahead of the enemy, he received a signal from the *Havock*, which was then with the disabled enemy cruisers some 50 miles to the eastward. It was timed 0020, and reported that she was in touch with a *Littorio* class battleship and had expended all of her torpedoes. Captain (D) altered course accordingly to 110° for this new attack and increased to 28 knots. A full hour passed before he received at 0134 a subsequent signal from the *Havock* to say that the battleship reported was an 8-in. cruiser and not a battleship. In these circumstances Captain (D) decided that it was best to hold on towards it and at 0200 saw searchlights ahead and, steaming through a number of survivors, arrived on the scene of the battle fleet's action and sighted the cruiser *Zara*.

British Fleet Night Action
(Plan 8)

The crowning attack of the long pursuit was performed by the battle fleet. At 2043, when the destroyer striking force proceeded on its quest, the battle fleet was left with a screen of only four destroyers. At 2111 Vice-Admiral Pridham-Wippell's report of a "stopped ship"[83] came in. The C.-in-C. turned at once to 280° and made for the position at 20 knots. The *Warspite* (flag), *Valiant*, *Formidable* and *Barham* were in single line ahead at three cables. The destroyers *Stuart* and *Havock* were stationed one mile to starboard, the *Greyhound* and *Griffin* to port. A light wind was blowing from the S.W., the sea was smooth with a low swell; there was no moon; the sky was clouded over; the visibility was about 2 ½ miles. Nearly an hour had passed when at 2203 the *Valiant*'s radar detected a "stopped ship" on the port bow bearing 244°, 8 to 9 miles. At 2213 the C.-in-C. altered course to 240° towards it, bringing the ships into quarter line. Radar signals were still coming in. In tense readiness the battle fleet held on its way. At 2220 the "stopped ship" was reported bearing 191°, 4 ½ miles. The destroyers on the port side were ordered to take station to the starboard, but the order had hardly been given when at 2223 the *Stuart* sighted a ship 4 miles off, fine on the starboard bow, bearing 250°, and gave the Night Alarm, which however did not reach the C.-in-C. before two minutes later the massive outlines of darkened ships were seen by the Chief of Staff and the C.-in-C. himself looming though the night. Two large cruisers could be made out on the starboard bow with a smaller vessel ahead of them. These were the *Zara* and *Fiume* returning to help the *Pola*. They were in a single line, with a destroyer ahead of them and two or three destroyers astern. They were steering about 130° some 4,000 yards off. The next few minutes were decisive. The C.-in-C. altered course to starboard[84] bringing the fleet again into single line ahead. Almost at the same time the *Greyhound*, which was then drawing ahead, opened her searchlight. Its beam fell right across the water, most valuably illuminating a cruiser[85] without revealing the position of our battleships. The *Formidable* being obviously of no value in a gun action, hauled out of line to starboard.

The *Warspite*'s turrets opened fire,[86] followed almost immediately by the *Valiant*'s. A salvo of 15-in. shells crashed into the *Fiume*. Her after turret was blown overboard; she listed heavily to starboard and burst into a sea of flame.[87] She was driven out of the line and seems to have sunk or blown up about 30 minutes later.[88] Searchlights were training on to the *Zara* and the *Warspite* and *Valiant* shifted their fire to her.[89]

Just before the enemy cruisers were sighted the *Barham*, in the rear of the line, had sighted the *Pola* on the port quarter making identification signals[90] and had trained her turrets on to her. When the *Greyhound*'s searchlight shone out, the *Barham* trained forward at once, opening fire on the leading ship.[91] A brilliant orange flash shot up under the bridge and bursts were seen along the whole length of the ship, which turned to starboard and made off to the westward making smoke. The *Barham* then shifted to the *Zara*. The latter had been heavily hit[91] and a big explosion forward hurled one of her turrets overboard. The action lasted barely five minutes, shell after shell crashing into the Italian ships, which were caught unprepared with their guns for and aft.[93]

At 2231 the Italian destroyers turned towards the British battleships and one of them fired torpedoes; to avoid them the battle fleet at 2232 ½ made an emergency turn of 90° to starboard. The *Warspite*'s 6-in. guns were ordered at 2232m. 40s. to shift target to a destroyer illuminated by searchlights but, having difficulty in finding it, fired only one salvo (2233m. 35s.), which fortunately did not hit, although straddling the destroyer, which turned out to be the *Havock* not having switched on her fighting lights.

The Italian cruisers were lying completely crippled and burning and at 2238 the C.-in-C. ordered the destroyers to finish them off.

A "night alarm" signal[94] had come in from both VALF and Captain (D), and the C.-in-C. being under the impression that their forces were in contact with the remainder of the enemy fleet, made a signal at 2312 ordering all forces not engaged in sinking the enemy to retire north-east "to ensure withdrawal on parallel tracks, clear of the destroyer mêlée". The night action, which had been startlingly brief and decisive, was over.

Plan 9

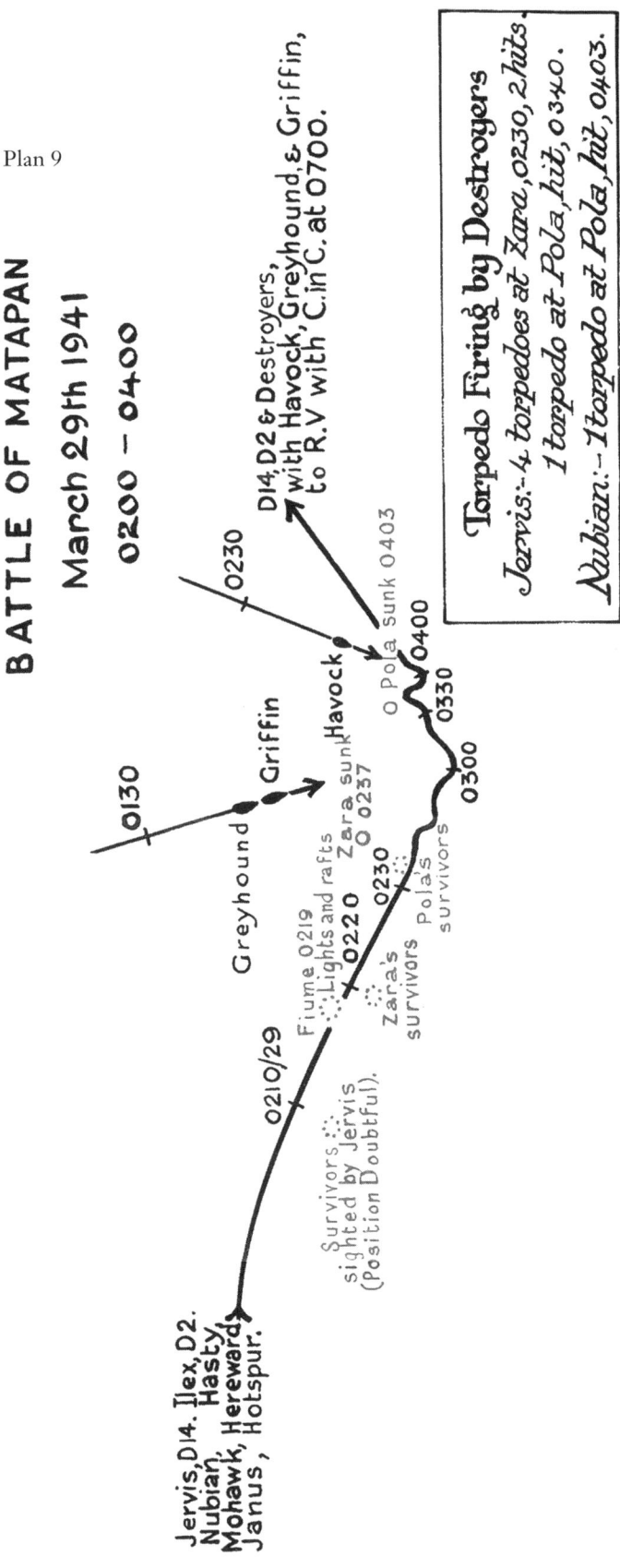

BATTLE OF MATAPAN
March 29th 1941
0200 – 0400

Torpedo Firing by Destroyers
Jervis:- 4 torpedoes at Zara, 0230, 2 hits.
1 torpedo at Pola, hit, 0340.
Nubian:- 1 torpedo at Pola, hit, 0403.

MOVEMENTS OF THE DESTROYER STRIKING FORCE,
(14TH AND 2ND D.F.)

ZONE TIME -2.

The Destroyers with HMAS *Stuart*
(Plan 8)

As the battle fleet turned north the *Stuart* was about to attack the enemy cruisers when three enemy destroyers[95] were sighted steering to the westward. The *Griffin* and *Greyhound* went off in pursuit while the *Stuart* and *Havock* proceeded south in search of the enemy cruisers. It was then 2240. A minute later came a signal from the C.-in-C. to finish off the enemy bearing 165° and the *Stuart* and *Havock* proceeded on this mission. At 2259 a burning and apparently stationary Italian cruiser could be seen about 2 miles to the southward with what appeared to be another large cruiser circling slowly round her. The *Stuart* fired her whole outfit of eight torpedoes at the pair and observed a "dim explosion" low down on the "non-burning" one. The *Havock* did not fire, being unable to make out a suitable target. It was then 2301. The *Stuart* opened fire on the burning ship and then went off after the other and found her at 2305, about 1½ miles off, with a heavy list and stopped. Fire was opened and two salvoes caused a big explosion and fires and by the light of the flames she was seen to be of the *Zara* class. A ship suddenly loomed up on the port bow passing very close and the *Stuart* had to turn to port to avoid collision, and as she passed down the starboard side only 150 yards away, an explosion in the "cruiser" showed her to be a *Grecale* class destroyer[96] "apparently undamaged". The *Stuart* fired two salvoes at her and the *Havock*, following up, lost touch with the *Stuart* and fired four torpedoes at her of which one scored a hit. The *Stuart* sighting another "cruiser"[97] went off to the south-west. The *Havock* continued to engage the destroyer with gunfire for "about twenty minutes", till she was awash and blazing fore and aft, finally blowing up and sinking about 2330. The *Havock* still had half of her torpedoes left. The burning wreckage of some vessel[98] (a cruiser or destroyer) could be seen with a number of boats and rafts near it. A large cruiser[99] was burning fiercely fore and aft, obviously about to blow up; another could be seen with a single fire abreast the bridge.[100] At the latter the *Havock* fired her four remaining torpedoes, all of which missed.

The *Havock* then turned northward at high speed and, returning towards the heavily burning cruiser, fired star shell and a couple of salvoes at her. The star shell illuminated a large ship resembling a battleship,[101] lying stopped. It was then about 2345. Opening fire on her, the *Havock* retired to the north-east, reporting it by signal as a *Littorio* battleship.[102] This was the signal received by Captain (D.14) in the *Jervis* at 0030, which caused him to turn back to the eastward to attack (See pages 65-68). At 0005 the captain of the *Havock* discovered the mistake and sent out a corrected report at 0030.[103] This was received at 0134 by Captain (D.14), who decided, however, to hold on to the eastward. "The mistake in the *Havock*'s signal," says the C.-in-C. "did not actually bring about any ill effect since the flotillas had by then missed the *Vittorio* and did useful work in polishing off the damaged cruiser."[104]

Meanwhile the *Griffin* and *Greyhound* had been pursuing the enemy destroyers. The *Greyhound*, after her opportune searchlight display, sighted the three destroyers in the rear of the Italian cruisers making off to the westward and gave chase with the *Griffin*. Fire was opened and hits were observed, but the enemy, turning southward,[105] were lost in the smoke at 2320, just as the C.-in-C.'s signal to retire to the north-east came in. They proceeded accordingly to the north-east until 0050 when on the *Havock*'s signal coming in they turned to the southward. At 0140 the *Greyhound* made the "Alarm" which turned out to be the *Pola* lying stopped on an even keel with guns fore and aft and ensign flying. They were considering "the problem of sinking, boarding or rescuing" when a challenge flashed out and Captain (D) in the *Jervis* with his destroyers arrived on the scene.

ITALY

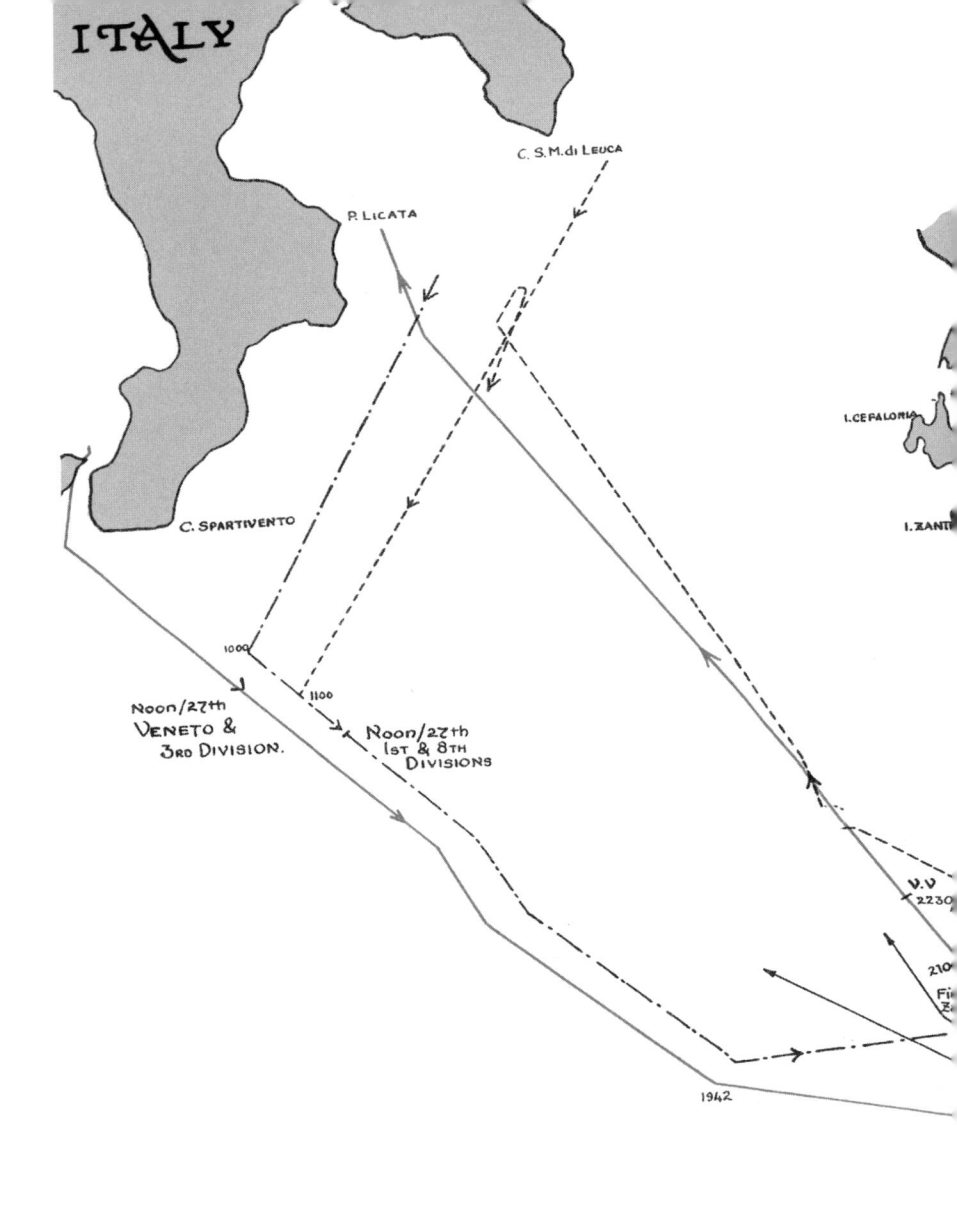

C. S. M. di LEUCA
P. LICATA
C. SPARTIVENTO
I. CEFALONIA
I. ZANTE

1000
1100
Noon/27th
VENETO &
3RD DIVISION.
Noon/27th
1ST & 8TH
DIVISIONS

V.V
2230
2100
1942

LEGGENDA

——— V. Veneto
– – – IIIᵃ Divisione
–·–·– 1ᵃ Divisione
····· VIIIᵃ ,,
——— cc.,T.T.
═══ Nemico.(i.e., V.A.L.F. with 4 cruisers & 4 destroyers).

Azione bombard...
Avv. navi. Avv. smg
Nb............Battleship
In ....Cruiser
Pa ....Aircraft-carrier
Fn ....D/F Fix

Plan 11

Italian Chart of Operations in Eastern Mediterranean
27th – 29th MARCH, 1941
FROM "GAUDO E MATAPAN" BY ADMIRAL IACHINO

For comments on positions reported to Italian C-in-C. by D/F or A/c, see Secⁿ 30(c)., and Appendix J. Adml. Iachino concluded that the ships reported by A/c at 1215/28, were, in fact in the position reported by D/F at 1315/2

The Sinking of the *Zara* and *Pola*

(Plan 9)

Captain (D) in the *Jervis* had sighted searchlights ahead, and, steaming through a number of survivors, sighted what turned out to be the *Zara*, with a few small fires burning on the upper deck. As he passed her he fired four torpedoes, two of which appeared to hit, and she blew up and sank. It was then 0240.[105] He ordered his destroyers to pick up survivors but not to lower their boats. Nine survivors were rescued by the *Jervis*. About 0250, observing a red and white recognition signal from the direction of the *Pola* about two miles away, Captain (D) stopped the rescue of survivors and proceeded in that direction. As he was closing he met the *Havock* who reported that the ship seemed to be on an even keel with a large number of men on the forecastle and in the water round her. The *Jervis* passed close to her; no visible damage could be seen except a small fire on the starboard side abreast her after turret. Ordering destroyers to pick up survivors in the water he proceeded alongside at 0325 to take off the rest of the ship's company. They seemed thoroughly demoralised, many half drunk and the upper deck in an indescribable mess. The *Jervis* was alongside for a quarter of an hour. At 0340 having embarked 22 officers (including the Captain), 26 petty officers and 202 ratings, the *Jervis* cast off, made an offing and fired a torpedo into her. As she appeared to settle very slowly, the *Nubian* was ordered to fire another, which completed the destruction of the *Pola*. At 0403 she blew up and sank. Captain Mack reformed his flotillas in single line ahead, with the 2nd flotilla on his starboard beam. Course was set 055° at 20 knots to rejoin the flag at the appointed rendezvous. The junction was effected at 0648/29.

Proceedings of Battle Fleet

At 2330/28 the battle fleet, leaving the Italian cruisers on fire and out of action, proceeded on a course 070°, reducing speed to 18 knots. At 0006/29 the C.-in-C. signalled his course and speed, and the position of rendezvous at 0700/29, ordering the *Bonaventure*, *Juno*, *Jaguar* and *Defender* to keep to the eastward until 0430. At 0430 the *Formidable* flew off three aircraft for a morning search between 160° and 305° while another was sent to search to the south-east for 30 miles and then to proceed to Maleme with orders for the aircraft that had landed there. Between 0600 and 0700 all units of the Fleet joined the Flag. None had any damage or casualties to report except one Swordfish missing. The searching aircraft returned at 0830 having sighted only a number of rafts and survivors. Two Albacores after refuelling went off to search the section between Messina and Taranto to a depth of 150 miles. At 0800 the C.-in-C. was in 35° 43' N., 21° 40' E., and course was shaped to search the scene of the action.

Between 0950 and 1100 many boats and rafts were seen and the destroyers picked up a number of survivors, a work which was interrupted by the appearance of German aircraft. As the destroyers had to draw off, the C.-in-C. directed the *Formidable* to send an aircraft with a message to Suda Bay to pass to Malta a broadcast message to the Chief of the Italian Naval Staff giving the position of the survivors still in the water. Including those rescued overnight the total number picked up by British ships was 55 officers and 850 men.[106] To hasten the work of rescue the *Formidable* was told to send an aircraft to a position 50 miles ahead of the fleet to transmit a call for rescue.

Force D and Greek Destroyers

Amongst the forces making for the rendezvous on the morning of 29 March was Force D consisting of the *Juno*, *Jaguar* and *Defender* which had been originally ordered to assemble at the Piraeus. At 0825/28, when the *Orion*'s first enemy report came in, Force D had made for Kithera Channel anticipating the C.-in-C.'s order to the same effect. Passing Kithera, Force D had steered due west at 28 knots in order to reach a position in readiness for a night attack. This intention was overruled by a signal from the C.-in-C. at 1323/28 ordering Force D to maintain a patrol off Kithera, which was accordingly carried out till 0430/29. The patrol was not entirely uneventful. At 1405/28 four Ju. 88's passed overhead on a course 070° without attacking. At 2055/28 two friendly aircraft dropped flares and "forced landing" emergency lights. North of Anti-Kithera Island, Force D, closing them, directed one on to Maleme and picked up the crew of the other (Albacore No. 5A of *Formidable*) unhurt. Both aircraft were making for Maleme after taking part in the dusk attack. Next morning at 0619/29 Force D joined the C.-in-C.

A flotilla of Greek destroyers had also been unable to take part in the actual battle. A request had been made for the Greek forces to be at short notice from 0001/28 and on 28 March the British Naval Attaché, who was kept informed of movements by the R.A. Alexandria, informed the C.-in-C. at 1215/28 that "seven Greek destroyers were proceeding at once through the Corinth Canal to await orders between Cephalonia and Zante." Unfortunately the word "orders" was received as "oilers" and the commendable action of the Greek Admiralty did not materialise. "These destroyers," says the C.-in-C., "had been sent through the Corinth Canal to Argostoli with admirable promptitude to a place where they were well placed to intercept the retreating enemy fleet, a task which they would certainly have undertaken with characteristic gallantry". On the other hand, though the issue was disappointing for the Greeks, the presence of another detached force with which the C.-in-C. could not have readily communicated would have added to the complexity of the situation. The Naval Attaché, Athens, sent another message at 2347/28 to say that the Greek C.-in-C., was awaiting orders, but it was then too late to do anything and the Greek flotilla was instructed at 0350/29 to join the C.-in-C. at the rendezvous at 0700. They were on their way thither when in the forenoon of 29 March the C.-in-C. requested that they might be ordered to return to their bases as he was leaving the area. They picked up 110 survivors that night[107] and the next day, 30 March, on a report coming in from a Sunderland Flying Boat of having sighted 600 survivors the Greek C.-in-C. proposed to send three Greek destroyers to pick them up and asked for the *Calcutta* to support them. By that time the Italian Admiralty had been informed of the position of survivors and as this implied a safe conduct the C.-in-C. Mediterranean requested the orders to the Greek destroyers to be cancelled.

Italian Fleet
(Plan 11)

British Information of Italian Movements
Between 1220/27 March, when a force of cruisers was reported by a Flying Boat in a position 100 miles, 100° from Augusta, and 0722/28, when A/C 5B reported four cruisers and destroyers 40 miles 130° from Gavdo, the British Commander-in-Chief did not receive any information of the movements of the Italian Fleet. It was not until the forenoon of 28 March that reports – either from aircraft or VALF – reached the C.-in-C. in sufficient detail for him to appreciate what enemy forces were at sea; but from Admiral Iachino's book and survivors' reports it is now possible to describe the Italian Fleet's movements between the times mentioned.

Object of the Cruise
The general objective was given in paras. 8 and 9 of Admiral Iachino's operation orders, issued from Naples, 24 March, 1941 No. 47:–

> Para. 8. "Attack enemy traffic on the route Greece to Alexandria, passing westward of Crete."
>
> Para. 9 (d). "All merchant ships that may be sighted in the area to the west and south of Crete, or in the Aegean, must be sunk at sight. In case of sighting enemy warships they are to be closely engaged only if the relative conditions of strength are favourable."

(a) *Vittorio Veneto* and 3rd Division
The *Vittorio Veneto*, wearing the flag of Admiral Angelo Iachino, escorted by four destroyers of the 10th Flotilla left Naples at 2100/26 March, passing through the Straits of Messina at dawn on 27 March, when the 13th Flotilla relieved the 10th. At 0900 on 27 March course was altered to 134° at 20 knots, with the 3rd Cruiser Division (Vice-Admiral Sansonetti in the *Trieste*) and 12th Destroyer Flotilla stationed seven miles ahead; these latter vessels having left Messina at 0615 on 27 March.

(b) 1st and 8th Divisions
The 1st Cruiser Division (Vice-Admiral Cattaneo in the *Zara*) with the 9th Destroyer Flotilla left Taranto at 2300 on 27 March and steered S.W. to a point 50 miles, 120° from the *Veneto* at 1000/28, when course was altered to 134°, being joined at 1100 on 28 March by a force from Brindisi, the 8th Cruiser Division (Vice-Admiral Legnani in the *Abruzzi*) with two destroyers of the 6th Flotilla. This force of five cruisers and six destroyers was almost certainly that sighted S.E. of Gavdo by A/C 5B on 0722 on 28 March and termed by us Force Z. Their original orders were to pass through the Anti-Kithera channel at 0400 on 28 March, then to sweep through the Southern Aegean as far east as Karavi Islet (due north of the east end of Crete). If nothing had been sighted they were then to turn westward so as to reach the Anti-Kithera channel about noon, 28 March and return to Taranto or Brindisi. At 2200 on 27 March, however, the cruise into the Aegean was cancelled by order from Rome, and Group Cattaneo was ordered to join the other forces sweeping eastward to the south of Crete.

(c) Change of plan for Group Cattaneo
The Italian C.-in-C. attributed the reason for this change of plan to a realization by the Italian Admiralty of the effect of the Sunderland's sighting report at 1220 on 27 March, for although the *Veneto* and Group Cattaneo had not been sighted (so far as they knew), the *Trieste*'s division (Group Sansonetti) had been both sighted and reported, as a consequence of which the English authorities might be expected to cancel merchant ship sailings in the Eastern Mediterranean. As such a step would naturally spoil his chances Admiral Iachino argued that probably it had been thought advisable by the Italian Naval Staff to cancel the most dangerous part of the cruise, i.e., the raid north of Crete by Group Cattaneo, on the grounds of needless risk.

(d) British sighting of Group Cattaneo (Force Z) a.m. 28 March
At 0722 on 28 March A/C 5B reported a force of four cruisers and four destroyers[109], which was termed by us Force Z and was in all probability Group Cattaneo (i.e., three *Zara*'s two *Garibaldi*'s – which incidentally were very similar in silhouette to battleships of the *Cavour* class – and six destroyers). This force remained in the vicinity of the other Italian groups until 0900, when it turned northwestward, speed 25 knots, until 1700. The 1st Division (*Zara*, *Fiume*, *Pola*) then reversed course to join the damaged *Veneto* about 1830, while the 8th Division continued northward to Brindisi.

(e) Group Sansonetti (Force X), and the *Veneto* (Force Y), night of 27/28 March

At 1930 on 27 March the 3rd Division altered course with the *Veneto* to 098° at 23 knots, proceeding to a point 20 miles south of Gavdo by 0700 on 28 March, the *Trieste* at that time bearing about 8 miles, 100° from the *Veneto*. All three forces were then steering 135° at high speed to close a force of British cruisers that had been reported by A/C at 0635 in a position estimated as 50 miles S.E. of the *Veneto*.

Italian Information of British Movements and Intentions

(a) Interception of the Sunderland's sighting report at 1220 on 27 March.

The Sunderland's sighting report of the 3rd Division at 1220 on 27 March, addressed to the C.-in-C. Mediterranean, was intercepted and read onboard the *Veneto* and in Rome. The Italian C.-in-C. noted the difference between the reported course and speed and the actual, i.e., 120° and 15 knots instead of 134° and 20 knots. He regretted the northerly error because the inference drawn by us would inevitably be that the Italian forces were steering to the south of Crete for the purposes of attacking shipping. To correct this impression he altered course to 150° at 1400 for two hours, hoping further reports would then be made by our aircraft to indicate their route was for Cyrenaica, but this "proved a useless stratagem because our turn, although visible to the aeroplane, was not reported to Alexandria, since the Sunderland did not succeed in communicating again with her base, in spite of persistent calls from Alexandria for further information." In connection with Admiral Iachino's remark that their "turn was visible to the aeroplane" it should be noted that para. 8 of the C.-in-C. Mediterranean's Despatch states that "visibility was bad and the flying boat could not shadow". Surface visibility at sea is well known to be tricky at times and this is sometimes particularly so between ships and aircraft, where it is not uncommon for ships to sight the aircraft without being seen by the latter. An outstanding example of this occurred on 27 November, 1940, when, in a position 300 miles N.E. of New Zealand, an aircraft was searching for a group of German Raiders (*Kulmerland*, 7,300 tons, *Orion*, 7,000 tons, *Komet*, 3,287 tons). There was a slight haze over the water, which may have accounted for the aircraft not sighting the ships, but the machine was seen from the *Orion* at a height of only 500 feet.

(b) Shipborne aircraft

Shortly before 0600/28 the *Veneto* catapulted her aeroplane (an R.O.43) to search a strip 20 miles wide on a line joining Gavdo and Alexandria up to 100 miles from Gavdo, while the *Bolzano* sent her aircraft to search between Gavdo and Cerigotto (Anti-Kithera). The *Abruzzi*'s A/C was catapulted off shortly before 0800 to "spot" for the 3rd Division, but owing to bad visibility during the action accurate observation was impracticable. Before returning to Rhodes the *Abruzzi*'s machine signalled to the *Trieste* that some of the 3rd Division's salvoes were seen to have fallen short of the target.

The *Bolzano*'s A/C completed her search, and before leaving for Rhodes, reported that there was nothing in sight. The *Veneto*'s A/C reported at 0643 having sighted at 0635 the four cruisers and destroyers with VALF, steering 135° at 18 knots in a position about 50 miles 120° from the *Veneto*. (Actually the distance seems to have been nearer 30 than 50). The Italian C.-in-C. had intended to invert the course at 0700/28, as there then seemed small chance of encountering enemy shipping, but in view of this sighting report he decided to continue westward, hoping to make contact with our cruisers. At 0700 on 28 March the situation from the Italian plot appeared to be as follows:–

Italian Forces

Vittorio Veneto and 4 destroyers (Force Y)[110]	20 miles, 180° from Gavdo Island Course 135°, 28 knots
3rd Division and 3 destroyers (Force X)[110]	8 miles, 100° from the *Veneto* Course 135°, 30 knots.
1st and 8th Division and 6 destroyers (Force Z)[110]	14 miles, 045° from the *Veneto* Course 135°, 29 knots.

British Forces

4 cruisers and 4 destroyers	30 miles, 130° from *Trieste* Course reported at 0635 as 135°, 18 knots.

At 0728, the *Veneto*'s A/C reported the British cruisers steering 290° [111] at 20 knots; it then established visual contact with the *Trieste* giving *Orion*'s bearing and distance from her as 250°, 20 miles; shortly afterwards reporting *Orion*'s course at 170°, 25 knots, and finally, just before 0800, signalling that "the enemy has turned to 120°, and is in line ahead formation, I am making for Rhodes." The aircraft landed safely with tanks practically empty, having flown for over five hours in a single engined machine, encountering a certain amount of A.A. fire from us and much low cloud, rain squalls in Kaso Straits.

Contact with VALF (Fig. 1)
After sighting the Italian A/C at 0633 VALF turned at 0645 to 200°, 20 knots. This turn brought the *Trieste*'s Division at 0745 into sight astern, bearing 010°, 14 miles from the *Orion*, and at 0752 VA.L.F. altered course to 140°, 23 knots. Thereafter, and until that evening (28 March) the movements of the Italians were known to use through V/S or A/C reports. On the other hand, apart from his knowledge of VALF's cruisers, the Italian C.-in-C., remained ignorant of our main fleet's whereabouts until 2230 when he saw the gun-flashes of the night action 45 miles astern.

(c) Shore-based aircraft
Comprehensive arrangements were made for air operations by German and Italian aircraft during the cruise (Appendix J); but, neither for offensive nor defensive purposes did the results come up to Admiral Iachino's expectations. In fact, he complains at some length of the failure of promised air support whether fighter escort, bombers or torpedo aircraft and reconnaissance, particularly the latter.

Fighter Escort
With regard to the lack of fighter escort the Italian and German accounts differ. The Italian Admiral remarks that "no German or Italian fighter aircraft were over us during the afternoon of 28 March, notwithstanding the statement of the "Comando del X CAT" (i.e., Comando Aereo Tedesco, 10th German squadron, in Sicily) that at 1430/28 four Me. 110's had gone to attack a Sunderland which was in contact with us. None of our naval forces in any of the three groups ever saw those four German fighters."[112] Apart from the statement of the "Commando del X CAT" the Luftwaffe Daily Summary of 28 March, 1941 reports that "nine bombers and ten fighters were escorting Italian naval units from S.E. Sicily to near the vicinity of Crete." Also, on 28 March in reply to a signal from the C.-in-C., the Italian Admiralty informed him that German fighters had left Sicily to escort the *Veneto*,[113] but in spite of all these statements Admiral Iachino maintains that

his ships remained without fighter protection. The only instance recorded by us on 28 March of Italian or German aircraft interfering with British attacks appears to have been that of two Ju. 88's during the 1127 attack by the F.A.A. on the *Veneto*, when one was shot down and the other driven off by escorting Fulmars (See pages 44-46). "but," says Admiral Iachino, "the first I ever heard of this incident was when reading about it in Commander Stitt's book *Under Cunningham's Command*. In reality during the cruise to Gavdo our ships were never escorted by fighters, and it is of no little astonishment to us to learn now that during that phase of the battle there was at least one friendly aircraft in our vicinity."[114]

Bombers and Torpedo Aircraft
With air attacks on British ships there seems to have been the same gap between promise and performance as for fighter escort. Two torpedo aircraft (S.79's) made an abortive attack at 1330 on 28 March on the *Formidable*, otherwise on that day our ships were not molested from the air. On 29 March at 1530 12 Ju. 88's launched an ineffective dive-bombing attack on the Fleet returning to Alexandria. (See page 92)

Reconnaissance
The following list shows what information appears to have reached the Italian C.-in-C., from air reconnaissance reports:–

(1) At 1400/27 and 1445/27 March, Aegean A/C reported three battleships, two aircraft-carriers and an uncertain number of cruisers in Alexandria.
(2) 0635 and 0728 on 28 March the *Veneto*'s aircraft reported VALF's cruisers position, course and speed.
(3) Morning and forenoon reconnaissances on 28 March of the Gavdo–Alexandria and Kaso–Alexandria routes were abandoned on account of bad weather conditions; but an S.79, an S.81 and a Cant Z506 completed surveys of the Southern Aegean and northern part of the Gavdo–Alexandria route (i.e., north of 33° 40', 24° 15'). The Cant Z506 at 0920 sighted and reported a merchant ship in Milo and three destroyers (*Juno*, *Jaguar*, *Defender*) about 20 miles north of Cape Spada, 195°; "nil" reports were received from the other two A/C.

(4) At noon 28 March two messages reached the *Veneto*, (a) from Italian Admiralty, (b) from Comando del X CAT, both announcing that the aircraft carrier *Formidable* had left Alexandria and launched her aircraft against the Italian forces. Since the *Formidable* had not been reported by reconnaissance aircraft from Rhodes, Admiral Iachino considered that "it was logical to assume that the *Formidable* had only just left harbour and must therefore be very distant from us." Furthermore, in his appreciation at 1300/28, he affirms that "the fact that no reference was made to any other units with the *Formidable* gave me a sufficient guarantee that the battleships had not yet left Alexandria (300 miles off), otherwise they could not have escaped observation."

(5) At 1230/28 a German aircraft reported four British cruisers (VALF's force) but made no mention of any other units in the vicinity; "another fact," says the Admiral, "which led to the logical assumption that the heavy English ships were still in harbour." This, surely, must be regarded as a classic example of assuming that ships could not be at sea, let alone nearby, because an aircraft did not report them, for at the actual moment of this German A/C sighting report (1230) the four British cruisers were just making contact with our three battleships (bearing 040°, 12 miles) and the *Warspite*'s position was some 60 miles S.E. of the Veneto.

(6) At 1425/28 an aircraft report was relayed from Rhodes with T.O.O. 1215/28, locating "one battleship, one A/C carrier, six cruisers, five destroyers in 34° 10' N., 24° 58' E. Co 200°" which was 80 miles eastward of the Veneto according to the Italian plot. This report undoubtedly referred to the British fleet (Force A) consisting of three B/S, one A/C carrier, nine destroyers which at that moment (1215) were 20 miles S.W. of the aircraft's estimated position and steering 270° but Admiral Iachino would not accept it:–

> "I was not a little surprised, since none of our own or German A/C had sighted enemy units of heavy type so close to us, and the doubt was whether the signal was a bad mistake like that made in the morning when we had been mistaken for English ships ... I waited for further news of this force..."

(7) At 1504/28 Rome passed to the *Veneto* a W/T D/F "fix" obtained at 1315 of a British ship in a position 110 miles, 060° from Tobruk and 170 miles S.E. of the *Veneto*. "This ship was transmitting to Crete and Alexandria." The question now confronting the Italian Admiral was whether this 1315 signal emanated from a ship separate from the group sighted at 1215, as would appear to be the case from the difference in position (100 miles), or was it from the 1215 group which had been reported by the Rhodes aircraft in a wrong position? The answer to this problem turned on a correct valuation of the positions given respectively by the aircraft or W/T D/F; which was the more reliable? Such dire consequences followed the Admiral's ruling in this matter that it is as well to quote his words verbatim. "Was the 1315 message concerned with one ship, or a group different from that reported by the Rhodes aircraft at 1215, or the same one? It seemed strange that the English should have divided their capital ships into two groups at a distance of 100 miles from each other. On the other hand it was impossible to believe that this ship transmitting orders to Crete and Alexandria could be a secondary unit which had nothing to do with their battleships; it seemed more likely to be an important senior officer's ship. Furthermore, it is necessary to consider that geographical positions obtained by W/T D/F bearings are, generally speaking, much more accurate than those given by aircraft since these latter are derived from a position estimated from the course and speed of the machine, calculations greatly influenced by meteorological factors."[115]

Shortly after 1500/28 Admiral Iachino came to the conclusion that "the two messages referred to the same group of enemy vessels as that reported by the aircraft at 1215 but in the position given by W/T D/F at 1315, i.e., 170 miles S.E. of the *Vittorio Veneto*."

(8) At 1600/28 Rome relayed an aircraft sighting report, timed 1550, giving "one battleship, four cruisers, 12 destroyers in 34° 05' N., 25° 04' E., co. 030° at high speed." This was about 170 miles S.E. of the *Veneto*, and Admiral Iachino took it to be further proof that only one of our battleships was at sea (p.137 of *Gaudo e Matapan*). Force A at 1550 was some 95 miles, 280° from the position of the A/C sighting report and 70 from the *Veneto*, none of our ships were near such a position at 1550.

Events after 1500 on 28 March

Recording his conviction, reached at 1500, that some of the English squadron from Alexandria besides the four cruisers of the *Orion's* division were at sea, the Italian C.-in-C. remarks that "this section appeared to be comprised of one battleship, one aircraft carrier and some smaller vessels in a position very much astern of us. Given slower speed it probably had not the intention and certainly not the possibility of gaining the 170 miles between us." Having formed this opinion the Admiral's attention at 1520 was diverted to a more tangible problem, namely, the F.A.A. attack on the *Veneto*, which ended in that ship being hit in the stern by a torpedo and temporarily reducing speed to 16 knots (See page 51).

Between 1530 and 1900 the Italian forces steamed to the north westward, Groups Sansonetti and Cattaneo both being attacked by R.A.F. bombers from Greece (See page 52). By 1830, the 8th Division having been detached to Brindisi, the 1st and 3rd Divisions were formed in line ahead to starboard and port of the *Veneto* (Fig. 2, page 57). At 1800 the Admiral was shown an intercepted message addressed to A/C QP 8 stating that "the aircraft coming from Maleme would attack at sunset and were to select the nearest battleships as their target". All ships were informed of this message and arrangements were made to lay a smoke screen at 1915, just before our attack developed. As a result of this attack the *Pola* was hit at 1946 by a torpedo on the starboard side between the engine and boiler rooms. All lights were extinguished and there was a scene of general confusion. Steam was lost in the main engines, though it appears from the reports of some survivors that the electric motors for the guns were still working. An attempt to raise enough steam for slow speed failed and the *Pola* lay stopped and helpless, waiting for assistance.

(a) The 1st Division turns back at 2100 to help the *Pola*
During the afternoon of 28 March the view prevailing in the Italian C.-in-C.'s mind was that most of the British Fleet was still in Alexandria, and

that whatever part of it might be at sea was at a distance of 170 miles astern of the *Veneto*. A further and last opportunity for correcting this impression occurred just before 2000 when a message from Rome was received giving a W/T D/F position of an intercepted message at 1745 in a position 40 miles 240° from Cape Krio and 75 miles astern of the *Veneto*.

In all probability this message was a signal from the *Formidable* to Maleme informing the F.A.A. base that her third Striking Force had taken off at 1735, in which case the D/F "cut" was not much in error (12 miles too far eastward); but as in the case of the 1215/1315 problem the same train of thought led to the same conclusion, "the 1745 message could not be from the British heavy ships since, in spite of a thorough survey of the ocean by air reconnaissance, only one British battleship had been reported at sea with an aircraft carrier, etc". The fact that nothing was reported seems to have been accepted by the Admiral as evidence that there was nothing to be reported, and in the absence of any special warning from Rome he remained convinced that no menace from our battleships existed. "The 1745 message," he thought, "must have emanated either from one of the *Orion* cruisers or from a destroyer." A few minutes after reaching this decision the Admiral heard of the *Pola* being torpedoed in the dusk attack and, not being able to obtain news of how badly she had been damaged, he decided to send the other ships of the 1st Division back to her assistance. "At 2018 I order the 1st Division to reverse course and proceed to the assistance of the *Pola*, I consider that, if they carry out the order at once, the Division will soon reach the position where she is lying stopped. After examining the situation I have complete confidence that Admiral Cattaneo with all his experience and authority will take the right decision without delay. My order crosses a message from Admiral Cattaneo who proposes to send two destroyers to help the *Pola*. I think over this suggestion but it seems to me to be absolutely inadequate if it is truly desired to give any real help to the damaged ship. Above all I hold it necessary that the decision to attempt salvage or to abandon the cruiser should be taken not by her captain, but by someone not governed by reasons of sentiment, and who has the authority to take responsibility for such an important decision. A section of destroyers could not meet these requirements, whilst the presence of Admiral Cattaneo on the spot would give every guarantee of the wisdom of the decision."

Admiral Iachino continues to describe his reasons at some length, laying stress on his hopes that as the *Veneto* had stood up to one torpedo so could the *Pola*, and if she was able to continue then she would need stronger escort than two destroyers. "To sum up, if it was desirable to make a serious effort to help the *Pola* and not to abandon her alone to her fate it was, in my view, necessary to send the whole Division and not just two destroyers which could only expect to rescue the crew after having sunk the vessel. At 2038 I confirm, therefore, the order to the *Zara* to take the *Fiume* and *Alfieri* destroyer division to help the *Pola*, at the same tine informing Rome of what had happened. At 2048 the whole formation altered course to 323°, steering for Cape Colonne at 19 knots. It was probably this increase of speed from 15 to 19 and an alternation of 23° to starboard which accounted for English destroyers losing track of us, not a turn to the south as English reports claim. At 2053 the *Zara* passed a message received from the *Pola*, 'Hit by torpedo amidships. Three compartments flooded, forward engine room, boiler rooms 4/5 and 6/7. Request assistance and tow'. About 2100 the *Zara* signalled:– 'Request permission to reverse course and proceed to the assistance of the *Pola*', to which I replied 'Approved.' Shortly after 2100 I saw the two great hulls of the *Zara* and *Fiume* followed by the four *Alfieri* destroyers in line ahead passing us at 16 knots on course 135°. No thought occurred to me that they would have to meet dangers any greater than a destroyer or cruiser attack, the same as we ourselves might have to encounter."

The reasons why Admiral Iachino envisaged no danger to the 1st Division other than from destroyer or cruiser attack have already been given; had he realized that at 2100 only 45 miles instead of 170 separated his forces from our three battleships (not one b/s and one A/C carrier) doubtless he would have consented to Vice-Admiral Cattaneo's first proposal to despatch only two destroyers instead of the 1st Division.

(b) Loss of the 1st Division
Vice-Admiral Cattaneo in the *Zara* did not live to make a report of what happened to the 1st Division, but we know from survivors' reports that he led the two 8-in. cruisers and four *Alfieri* destroyers direct for the *Pola*. The destroyers were astern of the cruisers until nearing the *Pola*, when speed was reduced and the *Alfieri* moved up ahead of the *Zara*. None of his ships possessed Radar so that in the absence of destroyers in the van the Vice-Admiral was dependent on the lookouts of the *Zara* herself for warning of approaching danger. Enemy action with the main armament was not

expected, nor indeed would it have been possible since no equipment existed (for night firing with anything but the anti-torpedo guns (Appendix H).

At about 2225 the *Pola* fired two red lights which were answered by the *Zara* almost immediately as the latter came under fire. At about 2230, when the *Zara* and *Fiume* were in action, the Captain of the *Pola* gave the order to abandon ship, cancelling it shortly afterwards and ordering the guns' crews to action stations. At about 2400 a destroyer appeared,[116] illuminated her by searchlight and opened fire, hitting her twice, under the bridge and aft, causing fires to break out. Another destroyer approached about 0100 [117] and shone a searchlight on her. About 0300[118], four or five destroyers were sighted; one came alongside to port and took off survivors consisting of 22 officers and 228 men. The destroyers then torpedoed her.[119]

From the *Fiume* only 7 officers and 53 ratings were landed by British ships. Survivors stated that at about 2215 she was illuminated by a searchlight and immediately hit by a salvo of heavy shells which blew the after turret out of the ship. She listed heavily to starboard. The crew panicked and abandoned ship and it was stated that she sank within fifteen minutes burning furiously.[120]

The *Zara*'s survivors stated that they saw the *Fiume* caught in a searchlight and hit by three broadsides. The fourth broadside straddled the *Zara* and the next hit her causing a big explosion forward, which knocked one turret out of the ship and caused a fire. Many members of the crew panicked and jumped overboard. The Admiral gave orders for the seacocks to be opened and the magazines to be flooded and later for the ship to be scuttled, an operation which was evidently not carried out.[121]

Most of her survivors were picked up by British destroyers the next day about 1100.

The *Fiume*, disabled by gunfire and possibly hit by a torpedo from the *Stuart*, sank or blew up about 2300; the *Zara*, disabled by gunfire, was sunk at 0240 by a torpedo from the *Jervis*; the *Pola*, disabled by the Fleet Air Arm at 1946, was sunk by torpedoes from the *Jervis* and *Nubian* at 0340. Two destroyers were also lost, the *Giosue Carducci* and *Vittorio Alfieri*. The *Alfieri* may have been the destroyer ahead of the *Zara*, which was engaged by the *Barham*'s guns and sank about 2330; the *Carducci* being the one torpedoed by the *Havock* at 2314 (See pages 72-73). The other two destroyers of the 9th flotilla, *Oriani* and *Gioberti*, escaped; but *Oriani* was hit in the forward engine room by a 6-in. shell.

The Return to Alexandria

On the way back to Alexandria a continuous fighter patrol was maintained by the *Formidable* for the remainder of the voyage. It dealt effectively with a dive-bombing attack made by 12 Ju. 88's at 1530/29 directed mainly against the *Formidable*, which did no damage beyond shaking her by two near misses. One Ju. 88 was shot down, another was damaged and three fighters launched by A.T.O. gear forced four of the enemy to jettison their bombs. At 0834/30 an S.79 shadowing the Fleet was chased and shot down by Fulmar fighters. The Fleet arrived at Alexandria at 1730/30. A submarine had been reported and as the ships entered the Great Pass, the destroyer screen cleared the area with depth charges whose resounding explosions apparently created a profound impression on the Italian survivors.

The Commander-in-Chief's Comments

With regard to the employment of aircraft striking forces and to the movements of the cruisers and flotillas the C.-in-C. made the following remarks (Despatch, para. 9): "It had always previously been my intention if contact were made with the enemy's fleet to hold back the torpedo air striking force until the battle fleets had closed to within about 50 miles of each other, or until the enemy had definitely turned away. On this occasion owing to the exposed position of the cruisers it was necessary to launch the striking force unduly early.[122] Few things could have been more timely than their intervention but it had the effect I had always feared that the damaged enemy turned for home with a lead which could not be closed to gun range in daylight."

Referring to VALF's signal timed 1210 reporting that he had lost touch, the C.-in-C. comments (Despatch, para. 10) that "with the considerable chance which then existed of being cut off by superior force, and adequate air reconnaissance being available, it is considered that the Vice-Admiral, Light Forces, was correct in his decision to gain visual contact with the battle fleet and check respective positions before resuming the chase. His force had been outranged and outgunned by all enemy vessels with which he had so far made contact".[123] Commenting on the report from Lieutenant-Commander A. S. Bolt, D.S.C., in the *Warspite* aircraft, made at 1914, giving the formation of the enemy fleet, the C.-in-C. says (Despatch, para. 14): "The last report, however, showed that a difficult problem was before us. The enemy had concentrated in a mass which presented a most *Formidable* obstacle to attack by cruisers and destroyers. By morning he would be drawing under cover of dive bombing aircraft from Sicily. The question was whether to send the destroyers in now to attack this difficult target or wait until morning in the hope of engaging at dawn, but with the certainty of exposing the fleet to a heavy scale of air attack. Decision was taken to attack with the destroyers and follow up with the battlefleet."

Reviewing the movements of the cruisers after 1930, the C.-in-C. says (Despatch, para. 15): "Meanwhile the Vice-Admiral, Light Forces, was also faced with difficult decisions. As dusk fell he was drawing up on the enemy with his cruisers spread to maintain contact. In the last of the afterglow it appeared that an enemy squadron was turning back towards him which obliged him to concentrate his force. This was undoubtedly a right decision, but from then onwards every time he wished to spread his cruisers to resume the search he was foiled by some circumstance, not least of which was D.14's decision to lead the destroyer flotillas round the northern flank of the enemy before attacking."

The C.-in-C. has this to say about the red light seen at 2242 by the cruisers *Orion* and *Gloucester* and by the destroyer *Hasty* (Despatch, para. 17): "On conclusion of the battle fleet action the signal was made (2312) 'All forces not engaged in sinking the enemy retire north-east.' The order was intended to ensure withdrawal on parallel tracks clear of the destroyer mêlée and was made under the impression that cruisers and striking force were in contact with the enemy. Heavy fighting had been observed to the south-westward which supported this belief.[124] Unfortunately the cruisers were not in fact engaged and the Vice-Admiral, Light Forces, accordingly withdrew to the north-east.

He had sighted a red pyrotechnic signal some distance to the north-west 30 minutes earlier and was at this time about to spread to investigate. This red light signal was sighted bearing 010°, simultaneously by D.14, who, seeing it in the direction of the 7th C.S. and knowing from their G.A.B. signal they had seen it, forbore to investigate.

"There seems little doubt from subsequent analysis that this must have been the remainder of the Italian Fleet withdrawing to the north-west (see Diagram No. 9). I am of the opinion that the course I selected for withdrawal led the Fleet too far to the eastward and that a more northerly course should have been steered."[125]

Finally, the C.-in-C. sums up as follows (Despatch, para. 22): "The results of the action cannot be viewed with entire satisfaction since the damaged *Vittorio Veneto* was allowed to escape. The failure of the cruisers and destroyers to make contact with her during the night was unlucky and is much to be regretted. Nevertheless, substantial results were achieved in the destruction of the three *Zara* class cruisers. These fast, well-armed and armoured ships had always been a source of anxiety as a threat to our own less well-armed cruisers and I was well content to see them disposed of in this summary fashion. There is little doubt that the rough handling given the enemy on this occasion served us in good stead during the subsequent evacuation of Greece and Crete. Much of these later operations may be said to have been conducted under the cover of the Battle of Matapan."

On 1 April a service was held throughout the Fleet to give thanks for the victory and on 4 April H.M. the King sent the following message to the Commander-in-Chief:– "My heartiest congratulations to all ranks and ratings under your command on your great victory" (see Appendix E).

A Few Reflections

The Battle of Matapan is of particular importance in the technical considerations to which it gave rise. One of the most important was the necessity of ample strength in aircraft. The *Formidable* had only 14 T.B.R.[126] onboard; her aircraft crews had to carry out a dawn search, two attacks during the day, and finally the dusk attack, which meant a return journey of two hours on a moonless night carried out by tired crews.

Seen through the perspective of years the battle came at a time when on the coast of Libya the inshore squadron of the Fleet was striving against heavy odds in the air to maintain the communications of the Army along the coast. German troops were massing in Italy, an enemy armoured division was assembling in Bulgaria, and a grim attack was impending on Greece and Crete.

At such a time, therefore, an Italian success at sea would have seriously threatened the whole situation in the Eastern Mediterranean, but their mission proved a complete failure and never again did their main Fleet venture east of the meridian of Matapan. Expressed in terms of the boxing-ring the fight between the two fleets at this juncture showed the Italians to be well behind us on points. In November, 1940, the Fleet Air Arm had delivered a well-aimed straight left to the Italian battle fleet at Taranto, and four months later followed up with a right hook to the jaw by torpedoing the *Veneto* at Matapan, while the British main Fleet delivered a heavy body blow by sinking three 8-in. cruisers. For several months after 28 March, 1941, the threat to our communications from surface forces was removed, which meant that, in spite of heavy losses to warships and merchant vessels incurred during the campaign in Greece and North Africa from air and submarine attacks, we retained control of the great watergate to the East.

Some two years later (May 1943) North Africa was cleared of the enemy, and the problem of maintaining our sea route from Gibraltar to Suez consequently simplified. Although many an anxious day was to pass before this happened, along the Libyan coast, off Greece and Crete, in the Aegean and the coasts of Palestine and Syria, as well as the perpetual and pressing needs of Malta, it can be truly said that as a result of the victory of Matapan the British Fleet, supported, as time went on, by the increasing power of the R.A.F. – remained mistress of the Levant.

Appendix A

H.M. Ships Engaged in the Battle of Matapan, 28 March, 1941
Destroyers
(D.F. – Destroyer Flotilla)

    Force A
Battleships
Warspite   30,600 tons, 24 kn., guns 8 15-in., 8 6-in.
                     Flag of C.-in-C., Mediterranean, Admiral Sir Andrew B. Cunningham, K.C.B., D.S.O.
                     Captain D. B. Fisher, C.B.E.
                     Chief of Staff, Commodore J. H. Edelsten.
Barham   31,000 tons, 23 kn., guns 8 15-in., 12 6-in.
                     Flag of Rear-Admiral 1st Battle Squadron, Rear-Admiral H. B. Rawlings, O.B.E.
                     Captain G. C. Cooke.
Valiant   31,520 tons, 24 kn., guns 8 15-in., 20 4.5-in.
                     Captain C. E. Morgan, D.S.O.

Aircraft Carrier
Formidable   23,000 tons, 30.5 kn., guns 16 4.5-in.
                     Flag of Rear-Admiral (Air), Rear-Admiral D. W. Boyd, C.B.E., D.S.C.
                     Captain A. W. La T. Bisset.

Aircraft	13 Fulmars.	803 and 806 Sqdn.
	10 Albacores.	826 and 829 Sqdn.
	4 Swordfish.	

Squadron Commanders:–

	Squadron	
Fulmars	803	Lieutenant K. M. Bruen.
	806	Lieutenant O. J. R. Nicolls.
Albacores and Swordfish	826	Lieut.-Commander W. H. G. Saunt
	829	Lieut.-Commander J. Dalyell-Stead.

Maleme R.N.A.S.
Swordfish   815   Lieutenant F. M. A. Torrens-Spence.

Jervis (14th D.F.)   1,760 tons, 36 kn., guns 6 4.7-in., 1 4-in. H.A.
   Captain P. J. Mack, D.S.O., Captain (D) 14th D.F.

Janus (14th D.F.)   1,760 tons, 36 kn., guns 6 4.7-in., 1 4-in. H.A.
   Lieutenant L. R. P. Lawford.

Mohawk (14th D.F.)   1,870 tons, 36.5 kn., guns 8 4.7-in.
   Commander J. W. M. Eaton.

Nubian (14th D.F.)   1,870 tons, 36.5 kn., guns 8 4.7-in.
   Commander R. W. Ravenhill.

Hotspur (2nd D.F.)   1,340 tons, 36 kn., guns 4 4.7-in., 1 3-in. H.A.
   Lieut.-Commander C. P. F. Brown, D.S.C.

Stuart (10th D.F.)   1,530 tons, 36.5 kn., guns 5 4.7-in., 1 3-in. H.A.
   Captain H. M. L. Waller, D.S.O., R.A.N., Captain (D) 10th D.F.

Greyhound
(10th D.F.)   1,335 tons, 36 kn., guns 4 4.7-in., 1 3-in. H.A.
   Commander W. R. Marshall-A'Deane, D.S.C.

Griffin (10th D.F.)   1,335 tons, 36 kn., guns 4 4.7-in., 1 3-in. H.A.
   Lieut.-Commander J. Lee-Barber, D.S.O.

Havock (2nd D.F.)   1,340 tons, 36 kn., guns 4 4.7-in., 1 3-in. H.A.
   Lieutenant G. R. G. Watkins.

Force B

Cruisers

Orion   7,215 tons, 32.5 kn., guns 8 6-in.
   Flag. of the Vice-Admiral, Light Forces, Vice-Admiral H. D.
   Pridham-Wippell, C.B., C.V.O
   Captain G. R. B. Back.

Ajax   6,985 tons, 32.5 kn., guns 8 6-in.
   Captain E. D. B. McCarthy.

Perth   7,165 tons, 32.5 kn., guns 8 6-in.
   Captain Sir P. W. Bowyer-Smyth, Bt.

Gloucester   9,600 tons, 32.3 kn., guns 12 6-in.
   Captain H. A. Rowley.

Destroyers

Ilex (2nd D.F.)   1,370 tons, 36 kn., guns 4 4.7-in.
   Captain H. St. L. Nicolson, D.S.O., Captain (D) 2nd D.F.

Hasty (2nd D.F.)   1,340 tons, 36 kn., guns 4 4.7-in.
   Lieut.-Commander L. R. K. Tyrwhitt.

Hereward (2nd D.F.)	1,340 tons, 36 kn., guns 4 4.7-in.
	Lieutenant T. F. P. U. Page.
Vendetta[127]	1,090 tons, 34 kn., guns 4 4-in. 1 3-in. H.A.
(10th D.F.)	Lieut.-Commander R. Rhoades, R.A.N.

Ships not present in the Action

Force D

Juno (14th D.F.)	1,760 tons, 36 kn., guns 6 4.7-in., 1 4-in. H.A.
	Commander St. J. R. J. Tyrwhitt.
Jaguar (14th D.F.)	1,760 tons, 36 kn., guns 6 4.7-in., 1 4-in. H.A.
	Lieut.-Commander J. F. W. Hine.
Defender (10th D.F.)	1,375 tons, 36 kn., guns 4 4.7-in., 13-in. H.A.
	Lieut.-Commander G. L. Farnfield.

At Suda Bay

York (Beached)	8,250 tons, 32.25 kn., guns 6 8-in.
	Captain G. H. Faulkner, D.S.C.
Carlisle A.A. Ship	4,800 tons, 28.5 kn., guns 8 4-in. H.A./L.A.
	Captain T. C. Hampton.

At Alexandria

Bonaventure	5,450 tons, 32.25 kn., guns 8 5.25-in., 1 4-in. L.A.
(Cruiser)	Captain H. J. Egerton.
	Submarines (on patrol in the Aegean)
Rover	1,475 tons, $\frac{17.5}{9}$ kn., gun 1 4-in. (off Suda Bay)
	Lieut.-Commander H. A. L. Marsham.
Triumph	1,090 tons, $\frac{16.28}{9}$ kn., gun 1 4-in. (off Milo).
	Lieut.-Commander W. J. W. Woods.

Appendix B

Italian Ships Engaged in the Battle of Matapan, 28 March, 1941

Battishhip. Force Y,[128]   1 battleship, 4 destroyers (13th Flot.).

Vittorio Veneto   35,000 tons, 30.5 kn., guns 9 15-in., 12 6-in.
Flag of Admiral Iachino.

Cruisers.   Force X,[128]   3 cruisers, 3 destroyers (12th Flot.).

3rd Div.
- *Trento*   10,000 tons, 35 kn., guns 8 8-in.
- *Trieste*   10,000 tons, 35 kn., guns 8 8-in.
  Flag of Vice-Admiral Luigi Sansonetti.
- *Bolzano*   10,000 tons, 36 kn., guns 8 8-in.

Force Z,[128] 5 cruisers, 6 destroyers (9th and 6th Flot.).

1st Div.
- *Zara*[129]   10,000 tons, 32 kn., guns 8 8-in.
  Flag of Vice-Admiral Carlo Cattaneo.
  Captain Luigi Corsi.
  Chief of Staff, Commander Franco Bovelli.
- *Fiume*[129]   10,000 tons, 32 kn., guns 8 8-in.
  Captain Giorgio Giorgis.
- *Pola*[129]   10,000 tons, 32 kn., guns 8 8-in.
  Captain Manlio de Pisa.

8th Div.
- *Giuseppe Garibaldi*   7,874 tons, 35 kn., guns 10 6-in.
- *Duca Degli Abruzzi*[130]   7,874 tons, 35 kn., guns 10 6-in.
  Flag of Vice-Admiral Antonio Legnani.

Destroyers (13 in number).

Naples to Messina: *Maestrale* class, 1,449 tons, 39 kn., 4 4.7-in.

With Force Y[128] (4 in number)   *Maestrale, Libeccio, Scirocco, Gregale* (10th Flot.).
Messina Onwards – *Camicia Nera* class, 1,620 tons, 39 kn., 5 4.7-in.
Granatiere, Fuciliere, Bersagliere, Alpino (13th Flot.).

With Force X[127] (3 in number):	*Camicia Nera* class (as above).
	From Messina – *Corazziere, Carabiniere, Ascari* (12th Flot.).
With Force Z[127] (6 in number)	*Oriani* class (4), 1,568 tons, 39 kn., 4 4.7-in.
	From Taranto – *Gioberti, Alfieri,*[129] *Oriani, Carducci* (9th Flot.).
	From Brindisi – *Navigatori* class, 1,628 tons, 39 kn., 6 4.7-in.
	Da Recco, Pessagno (6th Flot.).

Submarines (5 in number).
2. *Dagabur, Nereide* – across the line Alexandria – Kaso Strait, distant 200 and 150 miles respectively from Alexandria.
2. *Ambra, Ascianghie* – across the line Alexandria – Messina, distant 180 and 140 miles respectively from Alexandria.
1. *Galatea* – in Kaso Strait.

Appendix C

Extract From C.-in-C.'s Despatch and Other Narratives

1. The Night Action; which Italian ship was the first target?

"The battleship night action presented no novel aspect apart from the employment of Radar, and the outstanding success of the indirect illumination provided by HMS *Greyhound*, but a curious contrast of opinion has arisen over the actual targets engaged. The technical records of the action show that HMS *Warspite* engaged the rearmost ship first, and subsequently shifted target left to the second ship in the enemy line (the leading ship is now thought to have been a destroyer).

"My own opinion, supported by the Chief of Staff, the Captain of the Fleet, and several Staff Officers, is that HMS *Warspite* engaged the leading 8-in. cruiser (2nd in the line) and subsequently shifted fire right to the rear ship. It is a point which cannot be absolutely decided until the full story of this action from both sides is known…"

(C.-in-C.'s Despatch, para. 16.)

Some light on this point is obtained from the following Italian accounts:–

(a) Survivors from the *Fiume*

"At about 2100 the ship proceeded astern of *Zara* to the rescue of the damaged *Pola*. Enemy action was not expected and the watch below were asleep at their stations… At about 2215 she was illuminated by a searchlight and immediately hit by a salvo of heavy shells. X turret was blown out of the ship and *Fiume* listed heavily to starboard."

(b) Survivors from the *Zara*

"*Zara* was leading *Fiume*. At about 2200 when near the *Pola*… speed was reduced and the two cruisers were almost stopped. Shortly afterwards *Fiume* was caught in a searchlight and received three salvoes coming from what was thought to be 15-in. guns. The fourth broadside is said to have straddled *Zara* at about 2230 and the next salvo hit causing a big explosion forward which knocked out turret one of the ship and caused a fire..."

Comment. As seen from the *Warspite* the *Fiume* would have been the second cruiser and third ship from the head of the Italian line; *Zara* the first cruiser and second ship of the line; the leading ship of the Italian line was the destroyer *Alfieri* (not a 6-in. cruiser as was at first thought). If *Fiume* was in fact the first ship hit, then fire would have been shifted left to the *Zara* as shown in the gunnery records. A careful study of the Italian Commander-in-Chief's book *Gaudo e Matapan* does not reveal any fresh evidence on this point, probably because his account of the night action is based partly on survivors' reports and partly on the (British) Admiralty booklet *East of Malta, West of Suez*. In his personal notes the Commander-in-Chief states that both he and his Chief of Staff (Vice-Admiral Edelsten) remain convinced that the *Zara* was his first target and not the *Fiume*.

2. *Warspite* Narrative (Despatch, Enclosure No. 4, Appendix I/1)

2225-30   Sighted darkened ship bearing 250° (Green 10°) – three cruisers and two or more destroyers astern of them steering about 130°.

2226-30   Altered course to 280° to open A arcs.

2226-40   "Alarm Port" Red 10° as enemy appeared port side.

2227-45   Third ship in enemy line illuminated by *Greyhound's* searchlight. Identified as *Zara* class cruiser. (*Fiume*.)

2227-55   Open Fire.

2228   First 15-in. broadside. Range 2,900, bearing 232°. This broadside consisted of six guns. (Y turret was not bearing.) At least five and probably six rounds hit; no overs or shorts seen. Enemy burst into vivid flame from just abaft the bridge to the after turret. Director Layer reported seeing shorts strike just above the waterline and another observer stated that the after turret was blown clean over the side.

2228-06   Open searchlight shutters. Starshell commence.

2228-10   First 6-in. salvo. Range 3,000 yards, bearing 227°. Straddle. Rapid salvoes ordered. Three more salvoes fired before the order to "shift target" was received.

2228-40	Second 15-in. broadside–eight guns. Again spotted as mostly hits, at least one "short". The ship was now a mass of fire from the bridge to the quarterdeck.
2228-50	Order received to shift fire one ship left to the other 8-in. cruiser (*Zara*).
2229-18	First 15-in. broadsides were fired at new target–eight guns, range 3,000 yards, bearing 186°. Spotted as straddled, one short, mostly hits, no overs seen. Ship burst into flames. Three more broadsides were fired between 2229 and 2232 at this target. Hits were observed in each... During this engagement a third cruiser,[131] which had originally been leading, was in transit with the target making off at high speed, under smoke.
2229-25	First 6-in. salvo at new target. Range 3,000 yards bearing 186°. Spotted as a straddle with hits observed. Rapid salvoes ordered. Three more salvoes fired before order to shift target was received.
2230	A destroyer astern of cruisers bearing 240° and steering to close battle fleet was illuminated by *Warspite's* sweeping searchlights. 6-in. ordered to engage. At this time 15-in. was firing on a bearing well abaft the beam and the 6-in. control position was heavily blasted. The E.B.I. illumination was put out and difficulty was experienced in picking up target.
2231-32	Destroyer seen to fire torpedoes.
2232-25	First 6-in. salvo at destroyer. Range 3,000 yards, bearing 240°. Spotted as over...
2232-30	Altered course 90° away from torpedo menace... Shortly before sighting the cruisers that were engaged some form of identification or challenge was made on *Warspite's* port quarter. It consisted of white, red, white vertical lights flashing.
2312	C.-in-C. ordered all forces not engaged to retire to the north-eastwards...

3. Rear-Admiral 1st B.S., Narrative (Despatch, p. 163)

Para. 5. "At 2228, enemy was sighted in *Warspite* and was made out to be three cruisers in line ahead followed by three or four destroyers; the leading ship appeared to be a 6-in. gun cruiser,[132] whilst the second and third were made out to be 8-in. cruisers. Simultaneously *Greyhound* sighted the third cruiser whom she illuminated with her searchlight. This searchlight silhouetted the two, leading enemy cruisers to the ships astern of *Warspite*."

Para. 6. *Warspite* and *Valiant* immediately opened fire on the third ship (*Fiume*) the former firing two broadsides and the latter one. Hits were obtained with all broadsides at a range of 3,200 yards and *Fiume* was set on fire in several places; she sank about 30 minutes later.

Para. 7. At 2227, *Formidable* hauled out of the line to starboard and apart from firing a few starshells took no part in the action. *Barham*, which had sighted the stopped ship (now known to have been *Pola*) had her guns trained on an after bearing covering *Pola*, but trained forward and fired two salvoes (one 6-gun and one 2-gun) at the leading enemy ship (6-in. cruiser – later known to have been a destroyer), when silhouetted against *Greyhound's* searchlight. Hits were obtained in both these broadsides and a large fire started between the bridge and "B" turret. This ship turned away to starboard and was last seen beyond the 8-in. cruisers, retiring on a westerly course and making smoke. The fate of this ship is unknown.

Para. 8. *Valiant* after firing one broadside at *Fiume* shifted target one ship left and engaged the second ship in the enemy line (*Zara*). The first broadside at *Zara* contained several hits and this ship subsequently received the concentrated fire from *Warspite*, *Barham* and *Valiant*, the two first-named shifting target on to her after firing two broadsides at *Fiume* and the 6-in. cruisers[133] respectively. Sixty-two 15-in. shells were fired at *Zara* at about 3,000 yards range and it is estimated that about twenty hit... *Zara* was completely crippled and was subsequently sunk by *Jervis* at about 0230.

Para. 9.   During the battle fleet action, *Griffin*[134] drawing ahead across the line of fire was straddled by a 6-in. salvo from *Warspite* but received no damage. No enemy cruisers were observed to open fire.

Para. 10. Meanwhile the destroyers astern of *Fiume* had turned towards and one was observed at 2230 to fire torpedoes at the battle fleet before making off to the westward. The battle fleet was thereupon turned 90° to starboard and the battle field was left clear for the destroyers. *Warspite* fired one 15-in. broadside at an enemy destroyer during the turn away; the result was not observed…

Barham Narrative (Despatch, p. 175)

At 2226 during the approach in quarter line to port, a destroyer[135] was sighted bearing Red 70° and the armament… was trained aft to bear on her; she then called up by white light and made a challenge by red Very's light. I was about to order the ship to be illuminated when (the signal) "Blue 4"[136] was made and… the *Warspite* illuminated and engaged a cruiser on the port bow… some time elapsed before the main and secondary armament could be put on the new target…

The first broadside aimed at the leading ship[137] was a hit, a brilliant orange flash was seen under the bridge forward near "B" turret and other bursts were seen along the whole length of the ship; the range of this salvo was 3,100 yards… The leading cruiser was soon obscured by smoke, and as she was badly hit I ordered the fire to be shifted to Number Two in the line which was then brightly illuminated… Six 15-in. broadsides were fired, none of which consisted of eight guns and 21 15-in. rounds were expended. Seven 6-in. salvoes were fired and 34 rounds expended.

5. *Valiant* Narrative (Despatch, p. 181)

2216	Sighted the ship being reported by Radar bearing 191° 9,000 yards.
2219	Signal received from the Commander-in-Chief "Train all turrets on 240°"; Radar was put on this bearing and picked up two ships bearing 260° 9,500 yards.
2220	Sighted two ships bearing 260°. Guns trained on.
2224	Altered course together to 280°.
2226-28	Right hand ship[138] illuminated by searchlight. *Warspite* opened fire.
2226-35	*Valiant* opened fire with 15-in. and 4.5-in. at the right hand cruiser, a cruiser of the *Zara* class bearing 230°, range 4,000 yards. This broadside hit. Immediately after opening fire *Valiant* illuminated the left hand cruiser, also of the *Zara* class, and fire was shifted to this target. The remaining 15-in. broadsides were fired at this target and all hit.

15-in. Salvo Record

Broadside	h.	m.	s.	Range	Guns	Target
1	22	26	35	4,000 yards;	4 guns,	target right hand cruiser, X and Y turrets not bearing.
2	22	27	22	3,825 yards	7 guns	left hand cruiser
3	22	28	9	3,675 yards	7 guns	left hand cruiser
4	22	28	58	3,325 yards	8 guns	left hand cruiser
5	22	30		3,225 yards	6 guns	left hand cruiser
6	22	30	41	3,475 yards	7 guns	left hand cruiser

Total: 39 rounds A.P.C.

(*Valiant's* times 1 min. 32 secs. slow on *Warspite*.)

6. Remarks on Gunnery Aspects (*Warspite*) (p. 171 of narrative)

    15-in. Target I. 8-in. cruiser – 3rd ship in enemy's line
        (a) Range 2,900, bearing 232°, 2 broadsides open fire, 2228. Enemy's course about 130°.
    Target II. 8-in. cruiser – 2nd ship in enemy's line.
        (b) Range 3,500, bearing 186°, 4 broadsides open fire 2229. 18 s.
    Target III. Destroyer astern of cruisers. Range 2,500, bearing 239°; 1 broadside open fire 2233.
        (a) i.e., *Fiume*.
        (b) i.e., *Zara*.

Results (p. 171 of narrative).

Target I.	8-in. cruiser – not less than six 15-in. hits and possibly some 6-in. hits. Ship on fire from bridge to quarterdeck.
Target II.	8-in. cruiser – some 15-in. and 6-in. hits. Ship initially appeared to be on fire but this did not persist as much as in previous target.
Target III.	Destroyer – possibly one or more hits unconfirmed.
Target IV.	HMS *Havock*[139] – one salvo, 6-in., missed right and over.

Casualties: Damage received, Nil.

Percentage of Ammunition expended (*Warspite*) –

(i) 15-in. 40 A.P.C.	5.55 per cent.
(ii) 6-in. 44 H.E.	8.6 per cent.
(iii) Starshell 36	16 per cent.

Appendix D

Sighting Reports, 28 March, 1941

Note:– 1. The Signals are taken from the copy of Signal Log of C.-in-C. Mediterranean Enclosure 2 of C.-in-C.'s Despatch (M.050301/41).
2. The lettering of latitude and longitude at that time was as follows:–
BK = 22° E.; HS = 21° E.; FR = 26° E.; GV 33° N.;
KL = 23° E.; LS = 34° N.; MB = 35° N.; MC = 24° E.
3. The following abbreviations are used in this Appendix:–
A/C = aircraft; B.F. battle fleet; b.s. = battleship; co. = course; cr. = cruiser; dr. = destroyer; F/B = Flying Boat; kn. = knots; m. = miles; p.c. and s. = position, course, and speed.
4. The cruisers *Abruzzi* and *Garibaldi* in Enemy Force Z had profiles similar to a *Cavour* battleship.

	T.O.O.	T.O.R.	
1.	–	0654	General from C.-in-C. Reference position of Admiral, at 0700, [140] GV FR 17 estimated. [Reference position 33° 13' N., 26° 13' E.]
2.	0720 (A/C 5B)	0728	A/C of *Formidable* from ditto. NR. 1. Emergency. 4 crs. 4 drs. bearing 320°, 12 m., co. 230. My position 324 GV FR 90. [My position = 34° 13' N., 24° 57' E. Position Enemy 34° 22' N., 24° 47' E.]

3.	0739 (A/C 5F)	0755	Immediate NR. 1. A/C *Formidable* 5 VV from 2QO. 4 crs. 6 drs. bearing 23° 10 m., co. 220. My position 304° GV FR 100, based on reference position of the Admiral at 0400. [My position 33° 56' N., 24° 21' E. Position Enemy 34° 5½' N., 24° 26' E.] A/C 5F's true position seems to have been 15 miles N.W. of the estimated.
4.	0746 (A/C 5B)	0804	A/C of *Formidable* from ditto. Immediate. NR. 2. 6 enemy drs. are stationed bearing 110° distant 5 m. from 4 enemy crs. Enemy has altered co. to 167°.
5.	0802	0824	Malta W/T from *Orion*. 3 unknown vessels bearing 9°, distant 18m., co. 090°, My position 121 LS MC 10 based on reference position of S.O. Detached Force 0700. [My position = 33° 55' N., 24° 10' E. Position Enemy 34° 13' N., 24° 15' E.]
6.	0805 (A/C 5F)	0854	A/C of *Formidable* from ditto. Emergency. p.c. and s. of enemy battle fleet (3 b.s.), 303 GV FR 104 210° 20 kn. (via *Formidable*). [Position enemy = 34° N., 24° 16' E.)
7.	0812	0827	Malta W/T from *Orion*. Emergency. My 0802, 3 crs. unknown number of drs. bearing 010°, 13 km., co. 100°. My position 127 LS MC 15. Based on reference position of S.O. of detached forces at 0700. [My position 33° 50' N., 24° 14' E. Position Enemy 34° 3' N., 24° 17' E.]
8.	0824	0832	Malta W/T from *Orion*. Immediate. My 0812, 2 Italian 8-in., 1 Italian 6-in. 3 drs.
9.	0835 (A/C 5F)	0847	A/C of *Formidable* from ditto. Immediate. Have lost touch with 4 enemy crs. and 6 drs. Enemy's last observed position 303 GV FR 10.[141]

10.	0837	0852	Malta from *Orion*. Immediate. My 0824, 3 crs. 3 drs. 034°, 16 m., co. 160°. My position 132 LS MC 23. [My position 33° 44' N., 24° 21' E. Enemy position 33° 57' N., 24° 31' E.]
11.	0849	0854	Most Immediate. *York* from C.-in-C. Order Torpedo Striking Force to attack the enemy crs. in position 127 LS MC 15[142], co. 100° at 0812. Enemy position 33° 50' N., 24° 14' E.
12.	0859	0918	Malta W/T from *Orion*. Immediate. My 0824. Enemy is altering co. to port. My position 141° LS MC 33. [My position 33° 34' N., 24° 24' E.]
13.	0903	0920	Malta W/T from *Orion*. Immediate. My 0859. Enemy's co. 300°.
14.	0905 (A/C 5H)	0917	A/C *Formidable* 2QO from A/C CN 3. 3 crs. unknown number drs. bearing 030°, 7 m., co. 90°.
15.	(A/C 5F)	0905	Immediate. *Formidable* A/C 5 VV from A/C 2QO. Am returning to base. p.c. and s. of enemy crs. 300 GV FR 94, 290° 25 kn. [Enemy 33° 47' N., 24° 21'].
16.	0915 (A/C 5H)	0926	A/C of *Formidable* from ditto. Emergency. My 0905. Enemy has altered course to 300°.
17.	0921	0927	Malta W/T from *Orion*. My 0859, 3 crs. 3 drs. 322°, 14 m., co. 265°, enemy speed 28 kn., my position 128 LS MC 33. [My position 33° 40' N., 24° 31' E. Enemy position 33° 50' N., 24° 21' E.]
18.	0930 (A/C 5H)	0935	24° 21' E.] Emergency NR. 3. *Formidable*. A/C 2QO from A/C CN 3. Total number of enemy forces sighted up to the present is 4 crs. 7 drs. Position enemy is 298 GV FR 90. [Position enemy 33° 43' N., 24° 23'.E.]

19.	0932	0935	C.-in-C. from R.A. (A).
			My appreciation, A/C 5F was reporting VALF and 3 enemy crs. as battleships.
20.	0936	0946	Malta W/T from *Orion*. Immediate.
			My 0921, 3 ers. 3 drs., bearing 320°, 16 m. co. 320°, speed of enemy 28 kn.
			My position 130 LS MC 28.
			[My position 33° 48' N., 24° 16' E. Enemy 34° N., 24° 3' E.]
21.	0945 (A/C 5H)	0949	Immediate NR. 4. *Formidable*.
			A/C 2QO from A/C CN 3.
			Am still in touch with enemy. No change in situation since my 0930. My position uncertain.
22.	0950	1008	Flying Boat "V" from 201 Group. Immediate.
			A 146 Shadow enemy cruisers and destroyers in position 33° 50' N., 24° 22' E. at 0921.
23.	0959	1005	VALF from C.-in-C. Important.
			Torpedo striking force on its way.
24.	1015 (A/C 5H)	1022	Immediate. A/C 2 TX from A/C CN 3.
			One destroyer bearing 030° distance 2 m., co. 135°.
			My position 300 GV FR 70.
			[My position 33° 36' N., 24° 47' E.; the destroyer was the *Vendetta*]
25.	1020	1041	F/B "V" from 201 Group. Immediate.
			NR. 3, A 147. p.c. and s. of enemy cr. and dr. 33° 54' N., 24° 14' E., 320°, 28 kn.
26.	1029	1039	Malta W/T from *Orion*. Immediate.
			My 0936, 3 crs. 3 drs. bearing 304° distance 18 m., co. 320°. My position 158 LS MC 4.
			[My position 33° 56' N., 24° 2' E. Enemy 34° 7' N., 23° 44' E.]
27.	1058	1105	Malta W/T from *Orion*. Immediate.
			One unknown vessel 002° distance 16 m., co.
			My position 281 LS MC 10.
			[My position 34° 2' N., 23° 48' E. Enemy 34° 18' N., 23° 49' E.]

28.	1059	1127	826 Squadron from A/C to *Formidable*. Immediate. Two battleships in sight. My position 281 LS MC 10. [My position 34° 2' N., 23° 48' E.]
29.	1059	1127	Malta W/T from *Orion*. Emergency. My 1058 two battleships. My position 281 LS MC 10. [My position 34° 2' N., 23° 48' E.]
30.	1105	1123	Malta W/T from *Orion*. Immediate. My 1058. 2 battleships bearing 000° distance 16 miles, co. 160°. My position 269 LS MC. 11. [My position 34° N., 23° 46' E.]
31.	1106	1115	A/C of *Formidable* from *Formidable*. Immediate. Position of 3 enemy crs. 295 LM SC (?LS MC) 15. Enemy course 320° at 1029. [Enemy position 34° 6' N., 23° 44' E.]
32.	1111	1130	F/B from 201 Group. NR 4. A.151. Enemy crs. and drs. position 34° 05' N., 23° 45' E.
33.	1135	1146	201 Group from Scaramanga.[143] Emergency. NR. 1. Position of 5 crs. and 3 drs. is LS KL, 5524. [Position enemy 34° 55' N., 23° 24' E.]
34.	1143	1200	201 Group from Duty "V". Emergency. V2 p.c. and s. of enemy, 2 b.s., 3 crs. 3 drs. 290°, 25 kn.
35.	1145	1400	201 Group from Duty "V". Emergency. 2 *Cavour*,[144] 1 eight-in., 2 six-in., 4 drs.
36.	1150	1233	201 Group from Duty "V" NR 1. Emergency. V1 p.c. and s. of 5 enemy crs. and 3 drs. LS KL 5524, 280° 25 kn. T.O.O. 0935. [Position enemy 34° 55' N., 23° 24' E.]

37.	1152	1210	C.-in-C. from R.A. (A). Following from Fulmar. At 1105 *Littorio* battleship and 4 crs. attacking our cruiser force in position 205 LS MC 10. Have shot down one Ju. 88. [Position 33° 52' N., 23° 55' E.]
38.	–	1156	General from C.-in-C. Enemy battle fleet bears 290°, distant 45 miles from me.
39.	1210	1244	Immediate V4 201 Group from F/B "V". Position of enemy is 34° 57' N., 23° 16' E., based on a fix obtained within half an hour of 1200. Enemy are in single line formed on a line of bearing 295°.
40.	1218	1240	201 Group from F/B "V". VV5. Enemy course and speed, 315°, 25 kn. 5 enemy drs. screening enemy battlefleet.
41.	1220	1229	C.-in-C. from R.A. (A). Attacked one *Littorio* class battleship escorted by 4 destroyers, they were engaging own forces to southward who retired under smoke. Enemy position 150 LS MC 25, co. 160°, speed 25 kn. Enemy cruisers about 20 m. to S.E.[145] of b.s. Think probably hit. [Enemy position 33° 38' N., 24° 15' E.]
42.	1232	1246	Important. V6. 201 Group from F/B "V". Enemy previously reported are 1 *Pola*, 2 *Zaras*.
43.	1301	1332	201 Group from Duty "V". Important. V9. p.c. and s. of enemy B F 34° 56' N., 22° 32' E. 295·. My position, course and speed 235-Spada ? ? ?
44.	1307	1313	A/C "J" and "K". (R) 829 Squadron from *Formidable* Search for battleship last reported in position 321 LS MC 9, steering 270°. [Position 34° 8' N., 23° 54' E.]

45.	1311	1431	Important. NR 9. 201 Group from F/B "V". Position of enemy 34° 56' N., 22° 32' E., 295°, 25 kn. My position 235° Scaramanga 73*, based on a fix obtained within half an hour of 1300. *[My position is 37° 20' N., 22° 20' E. This is in the middle of Morea.]
46.	1344	1505	201 Group from F/B "V". Position of enemy 35° 3' N., 22° 26' E. (21 ??) (300 ?), 30 kn.
47.	1350	1356	Immediate A/C "J" and "K". (R) 829 Sqdn. from *Formidable*. Estimated position of enemy battlefleet at 1400, 340 LS KL 25. [Position 34° 24' N., 22° 50' E.]
48.	–	1404	General from C.-in-C. Admiral's reference position at 1400, 322 LS MC 4. [Position is 34° 4' N., 23° 57' E.]
49.	1503	1533	201 Group from A/C Duty "V". Immediate. V12. 2 b.s., 3 crs., 5 drs., 35° 25' N., 27° 44 ' E. Enemy's course and speed 300° 30kn.
50.	1525 (A/C 4NN)	1536	Emergency *Formidable* A/C. 2 XW from A/C 4 NN. My 1515. p.c. and s. of Enemy Battle fleet, 318 LS KL 62, 270°, 27 kn. 3 crs. and 4 drs. are stationed on the bearing 250°, 25 m. from B.F. [Position, Enemy 34° 45' N., 22° 10' E.]
51.	1558	1607	*Formidable* A/C from ditto. My 1525. Co. and distance made good by enemy is 280° 10 m. Enemy has made a large decrease in speed.
52.	1646	1652	*Nubian, Mohawk*, (R) VALF D.14 from C.-in-C. Proceed ahead and act as visual link between VALF and C.-in-C.

53.	1700	1728	Immediate V.19, 201 Group from F/B V. Your A 167. Force A 36° 01' N., 20° 32' E. 310°, 30 kn. Force B 35° 14' N., 21° 20' E., 325°, 30 kn.
54.	1700	1728	T 9048 Duty V from 201 Group. Emergency. A.68. Search for battleships, may be with force in position 34° 42' N., 21° 47' E.
55.	1701 (A/C 4F)	1710	Immediate. *Formidable* A/C from A/C 4 NN. My 1525. p.c. and s. of Enemy bf 233 MB BK 13 R., 305°, 12 kn. [Position, Enemy 34° 52' N., 21° 47' E.]
56.	1730	1753	201 Group from F/B "V". p.c. and s. of enemy battle fleet (A) 36° 09' N., 20° 19' E., based on a fix obtained within half an hour of 1700, 300° 30 kn. (B) 35° 26' N., 23° 10' E., 325°, 30 kn.
57.	1734	1736	*Formidable* from C.-in-C. "Y" Report indicates damaged ship may be 15 miles 320° from where we make it.
58.	1746	1755	*Nubian* from C.-in-C., Reference position of Admiral at 1800, 120 MBBK 29. Your reference position at 1745, 116 MBBK 26. [Admiral's position 34° 45' N., 22° 30' E. Your position 34° 49' N., 22° 28' E.]
59.	1800	1832	Destroyers from C.-in-C. Damaged enemy battleship *Littorio* class, 292° 50 miles from Admiral. Co. 300°, 12 kn.
60.	1803 (A/C 4NN)	1815	*Formidable* A/C from 4 NN. Immediate. NR 7. p.c. and s. of enemy battle fleet 286 MBBK 22, 300°, 12 kn., 3 crs. are stationed bearing 180° 5 m. from enemy battle fleet. Enemy are spread on a line of bearing 300°. [Enemy battle fleet 35° 6' N., 21° 34' E.]

61.	1825 (A/C 4NN)	1835	*Formidable* A/C from 4 NN. Immediate. Position of enemy 3 crs., 4 drs., 269 MBBK 43 100°, 14 kn. New force. [Enemy position 34° 58' N., 21 ° 8' E.]
62.	1827	1830	Base W/T from A/C *Warspite*. Emergency. 1 b.s., 3 crs., 7 drs. in sight bearing 270° distant 10 m., co. 310°. My position 300 MBBK 25. [My position 35° 13' N., 21° 34' E. Enemy position 35° 13' N., 21° 22' E.]
63.	1831	1836	Alexandria W/T from *Warspite* A/C. Emergency. 3 crs., 4 drs., in sight 265°, 14 m., co. 170°. My position 315 MBBK 3. [My position 35° 2' N., 21° 58' E. Enemy position 35° 2' N., 21° 41' E.]
64.	1841	1844	Alexandria W/T from *Warspite* A/C. Emergency. My 1827, enemy co. and speed 300° 15 kn. Enemy previously reported 1 *Littorio*, 3 6-in. crs.
65.	1844	1847	Immediate Alexandria W/T from *Warspite*'s A/C. My 1831, enemy previously reported are 3 8-in. cruisers.
66.	1855	1857	Alexandria W/T from *Warspite* A/C. Emergency. Enemy are concentrating. Total enemy force sighted up to time indicated consists of 1 b.s., 6 crs., 11 drs., p. c. and s. of enemy battle fleet 291 MBBK 41, 300° 14 kn. [Enemy position 35° 15' N., 21° 14' E.]
67.	1903 (A/C 4NN)	1905	A/C of *Formidable* from 4 NN. Immediate. NR. 9. My 1825. Enemy 3 crs. and 2 drs. stationed bearing 330°, 3 m. from enemy battle fleet. 7 drs. are screening enemy battle fleet.

68.	1914	1915	Alexandria W/T from *Warspite* A/C. Immediate. NR. 6. Enemy battle fleet is in 5 columns. Reading from port to starboard consists of 3 *Navigatore*[146] 3 6-in. crs. 1 *Littorio*, 2 *Nembo**, 3 8-in. crs., 2 6-in. crs. A/S screen consists of 4 vessels.
68a	1915	1918	Malta W/T from *Orion*. Immediate. 2 unknown vessels bearing 295° distant 10 miles, course unknown. My position 285 MBBK 22. [My position 35° 5' N., 21° 34' E.]
69.	1920 (A/C 4NN)	1921	A/C of *Formidable* from 4 NN. Enemy's centre bears 310° 14 m. from 4 drs. in the van.
70.	1920	1924	Base W/T from *Warspite* A/C. Immediate. Enemy's course and speed 295°, 15 kn.
71.	1930	1934	Base W/T from *Warspite*'s A/C. Enemy's course and speed 230° 15 kn.
72.	1930	1941	Malta W/T from *Orion*. Immediate. Enemy engaging our aircraft and making smoke, bearing and distance 309°, 9 m. Am concentrating, my position 284 MBBK 30. [My position 35° 8' N., 21° 25' E.]
73.	1950	2013	Immediate. Malta W/T from *Orion*. Searchlights and flashes 285°, 12 m. My position 290 MBBK 37. [My position 35° 13' N., 21° 18' E.]
74.	2037	2047	Immediate. 14th D.F., 2nd D.F. from C.-in-C. Destroyer Flotillas attack enemy battle fleet with torpedoes. Estimated bearing and distance of centre of enemy battle fleet from Admiral, 286°, 33 miles at 2030. Enemy course and speed 295°, 13 kn.
75.	2040	2100	Malta W/T from *Orion*. Immediate. One unknown ship 240°, 5 m., apparently stopped. My position 013 MBHS 21. [My position 35° 20' N, 21° 6' E.]

76.	2059	2113	Malta W/T from *Orion*. Immediate. My p.c. and s., 013 MBHS 25, 310° 15 kn., based on Admiral's 1800 reference position. [My position 35° 25' N., 21° 7' E.]
77.	2115	2229[147]	Malta W/T from *Orion*. Immediate. My p.c. and s. is 005 MBHS 27, 300° 20 kn. [My position 35° 26' N., 21° 3' E.]
78.	2115	2129	Important D.2, (R) VALF, from D.14. Shall alter to 285° at 2200. Confirm. My intention is to pass to starboard of enemy and attack enemy from the van. My p.c. and s. 033 MBHS 22, 300° 28 kn. [My position 35° 19' N., 21° 15' E.]
79.	2155	2242	VALF from *Ajax*. Three unknown ships bearing between 190° and 252° distance 5m. My position 348 MBHS 33. [My position 35° 32' N., 20° 52' E.]
80.	2215	2227	Malta W/T from *Orion*. Immediate. My p.c. and s. is 342 MBHS 41, 340°, 20 kn. Am keeping clear to North of own flotillas. All cruisers in company. [My position 35° 38' N., 20° 44' E.]
81.	–	2203	From *Valiant*. Surface craft detected by Radar 244°, 8 m.
82.	–	2214	Battle fleet from C.-in-C. Alter course together 40° to port[148], 240°.
83.	–	2219	From C.-in-C. Train all turrets on 240°.
84.	–	2220	Destroyers from C.-in-C. Destroyers on port side take station on starboard side.
85.	–	2223	C.-in-C. from D. 10 (*Stuart*). Night Alarm bearing 250°.
86.	–	2225	Battle fleet from C.-in-C. Alter course together 40° to starboard.

87.	–	2243	D.2 from D.14.
			Emergency. Alarm bearing 010°.
88.	2244	2245	*Gloucester* 7th C.S. from VALF
			Night Alarm bearing 320°.
			My position 342 MBHS 51.
			[My position 35° 47' N., 20° 41' E.]
89.	–	2246	C.-in-C. from D.14.
			Negative alarm bearing 010°.
90.	2312	2317	Mediterranean Fleet I/C from C.-in-C. Immediate. All forces not engaged in sinking the enemy retire North East.
91.	2322	2325	C.-in-C. from D.14.
			Your 2312. Do you include me?
92.	2326	2337	D.14 from C.-in-C. Immediate.
			Your 2322. After your attack.
93.	0020	0131	D.14, C.-in-C., from *Havock*.
			In contact with one *Littorio* class who appears undamaged and stopped. Will not return. Have expended all torpedoes.
94.	0030	0131	D.14, C.-in-C., from *Havock*. Immediate.
			My 0020. For 1 *Littorio* read one 8-in. cr. Heavy cruisers were in the vicinity. My position 036 MBHS 59. Am returning to shadow.
			[My position 35° 47' N., 21° 42' E.]
95.	0050	0058	D.14, (R) C.-in-C. from *Havock*.
			My position is 014 MBHS 18.
			[My position 35° 17' N., 21° 6' E.]

Appendix E

Messages of Appreciation

The following message was received by the C.-in-C. through the Admiralty from H.M. The King:–

> "My heartiest congratulations to all ranks and ratings under your command on your great victory." (2118/1/4/41).

The C.-in-C. expressed his satisfaction on the conduct of operations in the following General Signal to the Fleet (1131/30/3):–

> "The operations just concluded have given us a notable success over the enemy. The skilful handling of our cruisers and the untiring efforts of the Fleet Air Arm kept me well informed of the enemy movements, and the well pressed home attacks of the T/B aircraft on the *Littorio* so reduced the speed of the enemy fleet that we were able to gain contact during the night and inflict heavy damage. The devastating results of the battleship's fire are an ample reward for the months of patient training. This work was completed by the destroyers in the admirable way we have come to expect from them. The contribution of the engine room departments to this success cannot be over-emphasised. Their work, not only in keeping their ships steaming at high speed for long periods but in the work of maintenance under most difficult conditions, has been most praiseworthy.
>
> "I am very grateful to all in the Fleet for their support on this and all other occasions. Well done."

The C.-in-C. also sent appropriate messages of appreciation to the A.O. C.-in-C. Middle East, the H.Q. B.A.F., Greece, and No. 1 Group R.A.F. (1916/30/3) concerning the work of the R.A.F., and to the Minister of

Aircraft Production (1840/2/4/41) for the workers who constructed the aircraft employed in the operations of 27–30 March.

Messages of congratulation on the Battle of Matapan were also received by the C.-in-C. from the Prime Minister and the House of Commons. From the Prime Minister:–

> "War Cabinet desire me to express to you our admiration of the brilliant victory gained in the Mediterranean by conduct and proficiency of officers and men of your Fleet and the Fleet Air Arm under your own skilful and audacious leadership.
>
> We also express our gratitude to Squadrons of the Royal Air Force who so intimately and effectively prepared aided and confirmed the success of these memorable encounters." (Admiralty 0216/31/3.)

From the House of Commons:–

> "That this House on the occasion of the recent victory by sea, land and air, in North Africa, Greece and the Mediterranean, records with gratitude its high appreciation of the services of all ranks of H.M. Forces in those brilliant operations."

also from the Chief of the Greek Naval Staff and many others.

From C.-in-C. Mediterranean.	To A.O. C.-in-C., M.E.,
	H.Q., B.A.F., Greece,
T.O.O. 1916/30/3/41.	201 Group, R.A.F.

> "We have obtained a success over the enemy in which the Royal Air Force played a notable part. The extent and accuracy of the flying boat reconnaissance under conditions of whose difficulty I am well aware was a large factor in our being able to bring the enemy to action and is yet another example of the response 201 Group always makes to our requirements. The timely bombing of the enemy surface forces by the Blenheims from Greece was also of the greatest assistance in damaging and harassing the enemy and in giving him a dose of what he serves out from his own shore bases. I am most grateful to you all."

From C.-in-C., Mediterranean.   To Admiralty, 828,
                                    (R) R.A.A., H.Q. R.A.F. M.E.,
T.O.O. 1840/ 2/4/41.   H.Q. B.A.F., Greece,
                                          201 Group. R.A.F

"Please pass following to Minister of Aircraft Production. Begins:–

'The men and women who make aircraft for the Royal Navy and Royal Air Force have the satisfaction of knowing that they provided a most valuable contribution to the recent naval victory in the Mediterranean. The splendid aircraft you make, by finding, attacking and crippling enemy vessels, played a vital part in bringing the Italian Fleet to battle and defeat. I send my thanks to you all for your devotion and skilled workmanship which so materially helped the Navy to do a good job.' Ends."

Appendix F

Replies to Italian Questions on Phases of the Battle of Matapan, 28 March, 1941
(Ref. No. 65/FOLI/6/62 of 17 May, 1947, para. 2 – A to H.)

(A) Question At what time, of which day, and from which ports, did the British units which took part in the day and the night actions, put to sea?

Reply

The British Forces

Force A	Battleships	3	HMS *Warspite*, Flag of Admiral Sir Andrew B. Cunningham, K.C.B., D.S.O. HMS *Barham*, Flag of Rear-Admiral H. B. Rawlings, O.B.E. HMS *Valiant*.
	Aircraft Carrier	1	HMS *Formidable*, Flag of Rear-Admiral D. W. Boyd, O.B.E., D.S.C.
	Destroyers	4	HMS *Jervis* (D.14), *Janus*, *Mohawk*, *Nubian*.
Force B	Cruisers	4	HMS *Orion*, Flag of Vice-Admiral H. D. Pridham-Wippel, C.B., C.V.O. HMS *Ajax*, *Perth*, *Gloucester*.
	Destroyers	4	HMS *Ilex*, *Hasty*, *Hereward*, *Vendetta*.
Force C	Destroyers	5	HMS *Stuart*, *Greyhound*, *Griffin*, *Hotspur*, *Havock*.

Forces A and C Left Alexandria at 1900 on 27 March, Course 300°, 20 knots.

Force B Left Piraeus at 1300 on 27 March and passed southward through the Aegean to a position 30 miles south of Gavdo Island (south of Crete) by 0630 on 28 March. [N·.B.–Two of the destroyers came from Suda Bay.]

The sailing of the Fleet was due to a report from a British flying boat at noon on 27 March stating that a force of enemy cruisers and destroyers had then been sighted approximately 100 miles S.E. of Augusta, steering 120°.

(B) Question   What was the position and composition of the British formations at 0635 on 28 March, 1941?

Reply   At 0635 on 28 March the position and composition of the British forces were as follows:–

Forces A and C	3 battleships 1 aircraft carrier 9 destroyers	32° 40' N. 26° 35' E. Course 310° 16 knots	Approx 150 miles from Force B
Force B	4 cruisers 4 destroyers	34° 20' N. 24° 15' E. Course 130° 18 knots	

At 0645 on 28 March Force B altered course to 200°, having sighted an Italian R.O.43 and wishing to steer away from the direction of probable reconnaissance. At 0752 Force B altered course to 140°, speed 23 knots, increasing at 0755 to 28 knots. At 0802 Force B reported their position and that of an enemy cruiser force to the Commander-in-Chief, Mediterranean. At 0812 the enemy opened fire, and a running fight continued until 0855 when the enemy turned round to the N.W. and Force B followed them.

(C) Question   How was the British Naval Force at sea sub-divided at 1930/28 March?

Reply

Battleships	3	HMS *Warspite, Valiant, Formidable, Barham* formed in single line ahead, 3 cables apart. Course 300°, 20 knots.
Aircraft Carrier	1	
Position of *Warspite*:		85 miles, 195° from Cape Matapan and estimated 45 miles 110° from *Vittorio Veneto*.
Destroyer Screen (4):		HMAS *Stuart*, HMS *Havock*, 1 mile to starboard of Battle fleet. HMS *Greyhound, Griffin*, 1 mile to Port of Battle fleet.
Destroyer Striking Force (8):		HMS *Jervis, Janus, Nubian, Mohawk* – 14th flotilla. HMS *Ilex, Hasty, Hereward, Hotspur* – 2nd flotilla. Stationed 1 mile on either bow of battle fleet: 14th to Port. 2nd to Starboard.
Cruisers:		HMS *Orion, Ajax, Perth, Gloucester* formed in line ahead, Course 280°, 26 knots.
Position:		35 miles, 280° from the battle fleet. Reported at 1914 to C.-in-C. Mediterranean "Enemy in sight on Starboard bow."

(D) Question What were the courses of the British units between 1930 and 2230 on 28 March, 1941?

Reply

Battleship and Destroyer Screen.	1930	Course 300°	20 knots	Line ahead.
	2111	Course 280°	20 knots	Line ahead.
	2213	Course 240°	20 knots	Quarterline to port.
	2227	Course 280°	20 knots	Line ahead.
		(*Formidable* hauled out of line to starboard.)		
	2228/29	*Warspite*, *Valiant*, *Barham* (in that order) opened fire first on *Fiume*, then *Zara*.		
	2232	Battlefleet made an emergency turn of 90° to Starboard to avoid torpedoes.		
	2238	Resumed Course 280°. Destroyers ordered to sink damaged enemy cruisers.		
	2330	Course 070°, 18 knots.		
Destroyer Screen.	2240	*Stuart* and *Havock* turned to southward in search of damaged enemy cruisers; *Griffin* and *Greyhound* – proceeded westward after enemy destroyers.		
Cruisers – 4.	1930	Course 280°	26 knots	Line ahead.
	1932	Course 320°	30 knots	Line ahead.
	1949	Course 320°	20 knots	Line ahead.
	1950	Course 290°	20 knots	Line ahead.
	2014	Course 310°	15 knots.	Line ahead.
	2033	Course 060°	15 knots.	Line ahead.
	2048	Course 310°	15 knots.	
	2115	Course 300°	15 knots.	
	2119	Course 300°	20 knots	
	2202	Course 340°	20 knots	Line ahead.
	(2229	Flashes of night action seen right astern bearing 160°).		
	2255	Course 360°	20 knots	Line ahead.
	2322	Course 060°	20 knots	
Destroyer Striking Force – 8.	1930	Course 290°	20 knots	
	2040	Received orders to attack enemy, estimated to be 286°, 33 miles from *Warspite* and steering 295° at 13 knots.		
	2043	Course 300°	28 knots	Division in line ahead 2nd flotilla 6 cables to Starboard of 14th flotilla.

| | | 2200 | Altered course to 285°. |
| | | 2322 | Altered course to 040°. |

(E) and (F)

Question What was the time of sighting by the British of the *Fiume*, *Zara* and 4 Destroyers' formation? Was the sighting visual or by radar? Which was the first ship to sight the Italian Division?

Reply	2155	*Ajax*	Radar reported 3 vessels bearing between 190° and 252° 5 miles off.
	2203	*Valiant*	Radar reported "Stopped ship, 244°, 8 to 9 miles", Fleet Course 280°.
	2220	*Valiant*	Radar reported "Stopped ship, 191°, 4½ miles", Fleet Course 240°.
	2223	*Stuart*	Sighted "Unknown vessel, 250°, 4 miles", Fleet Course 240°.
	2225	*Warspite*	Sighted "2 large, 1 small ship, fine on starboard bow", Fleet Course 240°.
	2226		Fleet A/C into line ahead, Course 280°.

(G) Question Did the British Fleet sustain any damage in the action during the morning of 28 March?

Reply Minor damage to the *Orion* caused by a "near miss" from *Vittorio Veneto* between 1100 and 1110/28 March.
The Vice-Admiral, Force B, reported that the enemy's shooting at 32,000 yards was remarkably accurate.

(H) Question What was the exact composition of the formation which met with the First Division (*Zara*, *Fiume* and 4 Destroyers)?

Reply Time of opening fire – 2228 hrs.

Battleships	3	*Warspite*, *Valiant*, *Barham* Line ahead, 3 cables apart.
Destroyers	4	*Stuart*, *Havock* – 7½ cables on starboard bow of *Warspite* and *Barham*.
		Greyhound, *Griffin*[149] – 7½ cables on port bow of *Warspite* and *Barham*.

Appendix G

Italian Account of the Fleet Air Arm Torpedo Attack on the *Vittorio Veneto*, 1515–1525
(Extract from Admiral Iachino's book, *Gaudo e Matapan*)

After describing unsuccessful high-level bombing attacks by the Royal Air Force on the *Vittorio Veneto* at 1420 and 1450 Admiral Iachino continues as follows:– "At 1519 the third and most important air attack on the *Veneto* took place, conducted this time with particular ability and bravery by aircraft of the Swordfish type, which had evidently come from an aircraft carrier. It was a co-ordinated bomb and torpedo attack; the bombers keeping at high level over the ship while the torpedo aircraft came in immediately the former had dropped their bombs. The attention of the lookouts and the A/A gunners was thus diverted by the approach of the bombers against which they opened fire. Whilst everyone was busy with these aircraft, which appeared to be by themselves, three torpedo aircraft approached from astern without being sighted until very close. They kept formation at a low level, machine-gunning the bridges and upper works of the escort vessels so as to disturb A/A fire; they then flew ahead of the *Veneto* to about 3,000 metres and spread out, two to port and one to starboard, reversing their course and steering straight towards us.

"The attack immediately began to look extremely dangerous because it was very difficult rapidly to change the target for the A/A guns, which were still firing at the bombers; also, the machine-gunning had surprised and somewhat paralysed the A.A. fire of our escorts, rendering their efforts much less efficacious than usual. The three torpedo aircraft were thus enabled to steer towards the *Veneto* from three different directions without being unduly disturbed by our gunfire, and continued to approach with great speed 'head-on'.

"Under these conditions there remained as our only defence the manoeuvring of the ship herself, and accordingly I hastened to the voice pipe from the captain's bridge to order an immediate alteration of course. The captain had already thought of this, and I heard through the voice pipe his order to the quartermaster to put the helm hard to starboard. The morning scene (i.e., the attack at 1127) was repeated; before the ship began effectively to turn to starboard an interminable interval of time seemed to pass, during which we all had our hearts in our mouths and our eyes fixed on the aircraft. These continued to steer at top speed towards us without being seriously threatened by gunfire from the pom-poms and machine guns, which after some delay began to aim at the new targets. All three aircraft dropped their torpedoes at a relatively short distance; the aircraft which was ahead, but slightly to port of us, showed greater skill and courage than the others and approached the closest of the three to the ship before "dropping". We saw clearly the torpedo fall in the water not more than 1,000 metres ahead of us just at the moment when the ship commenced slowly to turn to starboard. We anxiously followed the track which could be seen clearly coming straight at us, and the next few seconds seemed like hours. The machine-gun fire became more intense and accurate against the aircraft, which having launched their torpedoes now sought to escape. The aircraft which had made the most daring attack had come very close to the *Veneto* and was in evident difficulty to gain height and get away quickly. In the end I saw him try a bold manoeuvre with the object of throwing off our fire that was now being concentrated entirely on him. He turned to port as if to cross our course and escape to the starboard side where the A/A fire was less intense. At the moment of his passing close across our bows he presented a full target to the machine guns, which were placed well forward and fired point blank at their target at short range. He must have been hit many times as the machine was seen to stagger and then dip violently across our track some dozens of metres from our bows, then fall at last into the sea about 1,000 metres to starboard of the *Veneto*. The bold pilot perished without having the satisfaction of seeing the successful result of his shot."

Admiral Iachino then describes how a few seconds after the aircraft had dived into the sea a torpedo struck the *Veneto*'s port quarter, and while everyone's attention was drawn to this event another aircraft dropped a bomb close to the stern, so close that a column of water from the explosion fell on the quarterdeck. He considered that the swing of the ship's stern to port that caused the bomb to miss at the same time facilitated the torpedo hit.

Before describing the dusk Fleet Air Arm torpedo attack Admiral Iachino concludes Chapter 5 of his book with some general comments on the day attacks on the *Veneto* as follows:– "It is necessary to recognise that the *Formidable* had performed a very useful service throughout the day, organising the three most dangerous attacks against us. The first was that of six Swordfish, delivered in the forenoon without success, at the end of the second phase of the battle of Gavdo. The second and most serious was at 1530, and in it perished the leader of the flight Lieutenant-Commander J. Dalyell-Stead, who so daringly succeeded in torpedoing the *Veneto*. The third attack took place at sunset. It is interesting to record that the morning flight had returned with the conviction of having hit the *Veneto* with at least one torpedo; the pilots asserting that they had seen the ship listing over and damaged by the explosion, whilst in reality none of these things happened. Also, in the afternoon the bomber which attacked us with a heavy calibre bomb aft returned stating that he had hit us and had seen flames and smoke rise from the point of the explosion. The sergeant-pilot was absolutely certain of having "made" his target, and affirmed, doubtless in good faith, that he had seen with his own eyes the bombs hit exactly the spot onboard the ship at which he had accurately aimed. This shows how frequently the English airmen committed errors of over-estimating the effects of their bomb and torpedo attacks. So it was with us; often our aircraft returned from an attack with the mathematical certainty of having achieved a success which was then denied by the enemy and their denials borne out by events. This state of affairs leads naturally to a loss of confidence in the reports of aircraft about their action results, which seemed highly exaggerated. In point of fact it is a phenomenon common to pilots of all aircraft employed in war, for it really springs from a trick of optical illusion interpreted perhaps too optimistically, although in good faith, by those who took part in the action.

"Anyhow, it is certain that the major successes of the day were achieved by the aircraft carrier, confirming the importance of the practical contribution which a unit of this type gives to wartime operations at sea, above all when the opponent is completely deprived of aerial protection, such as ourselves. It would have been sufficient for a small group of fighters over us to render the enemy attacks nugatory. Exposed as we were, however, to all the threats of the air our fate appeared to be definitely sealed."

Appendix H

Italian Arrangements for Night Action
(Extract from Admiral Iachino's book, *Gaudo e Matapan*)

"In the years immediately preceding the war much care was given to planning the methods of night action, as they were considered highly important and constituted a promising resource for a navy such as ours of inferior strength. But with us these methods were confined almost exclusively to developing and perfecting night torpedo attack by destroyers or torpedo boats, for a night encounter between major units was not thought to be a practical possibility. A division of cruisers or battleships would always be accompanied at night by an escort of destroyers stationed well ahead, which would give warning in good time of any meeting with the enemy, thus providing the chance to turn away and avoid a dangerous mêlée between the big ships.

"On the night of Matapan the larger units were keeping only the anti-torpedo boat armament ready for use, and those guns were supplied with anti-flash and reduced charge ammunition (so as not to blind the gunlayers), whilst the heavy guns had not been so provided since their employment in a night action was held to be improbable.

"It must be said at this point that for the execution of night firing by guns of large calibre it is necessary to solve not only the delicate problem of anti-flash ammunition but also many other technical points relating to the gunlaying and control of fire. Without going into long and tiresome details it will be sufficient to consider the necessity of the guns all bearing exactly on the same target so as to avoid a dangerous dispersion of fire, also there was the impossibility of achieving this object with our existing apparatus for gunlaying in daylight, which had not been adapted for the particular exigencies of night firing. It would have meant new apparatus, new communications, new adaptations of the control of fire, of rangefinders, etc.; all these things which naturally could not be improvised, and which called for much time for study and trying-out in peace-time.

"It was therefore with noteworthy astonishment on our part that we realised the efficiency in night firing by 15-in. guns of the *Warspite* type of battleship, evident proof that the English had, in their preparation for night action, followed a policy opposed to ours and had succeeded in solving the delicate problems connected with that form of firing.

"In the particular circumstances of the encounter off Matapan, the policy adopted by the English in their preparation proved providential for them, since the failure to have a night escort ahead of our cruisers brought about that direct and sudden contact between large units, which our Naval Staff had excluded from the field of practical possibilities.

"After Matapan all our ships in due course were fitted for carrying out night firing, even the heavy guns which were supplied with the necessary ammunition. But no occasion arose to try out in practice the efficiency of this new organisation because, until the end of the war, there were no further night actions between heavy naval units."

Searchlights

"Another matter of surprise on our part on the night of 28 March was the extensive and prompt use of searchlights made by all the units of the English squadron, especially the precision with which they at once illuminated their objectives, thus permitting the immediate development of a great volume of fire from all their guns. The question of the use of searchlights in case of night fighting had been discussed by us over a long period, and a definite decision taken not to use them; not because it was not thought useful to illuminate the target by such means but because our searchlights were not all of long range and principally because their means of laying at any distance were rather imperfect. This would often have meant, especially under conditions of rough seas with consequent oscillation of the platform, that the beam of the searchlight could not be maintained continuously on the target, thus obstructing rather than facilitating good gunlaying.

"Evidently the English had succeeded in solving better than us this important technical problem, and were accustomed to burn their searchlights immediately in any case of sighting at night, an act which had the very useful result of permitting them to open fire with the minimum of delay. It is evident that at the very short range of night firing whoever succeeds in firing first is certain of success, and also has every probability of destroying the enemy without himself sustaining serious damage."

Starshell

"Renouncing, as we had done, the use of searchlights gunfire could only begin when the target had been satisfactorily illuminated by star shell. These were fired, of course, immediately any suspicious object was sighted; but then at least 15 or 20 seconds must elapse before the shells burst at the end of their flight. Those 15 to 20 seconds meant delay sufficient to put our ships clearly in a position of inferiority with regard to the enemy who – as in the case of the English – were able to open fire immediately, thanks to the use of their searchlights.

"After Matapan we also tried to employ this means of prompt illumination of the target, but never succeeded in finding the means of laying the searchlight's beam with complete certainty on the exact bearing, as is obviously necessary. Finally, the star shell used by the English, together with the searchlights so as to obtain a greater and more extensive illumination of the scene of action, were a surprise to us because they seemed to have greater diffusion, a brighter light and to last longer than ours."

Comment

It is interesting to compare the searchlight problems of the Italian Navy in 1941 with our own situation in the early part of the first World War. We had not then overcome the same difficulties of laying and control as those mentioned by Admiral Iachino, and what was worse we found that the Germans were ahead of us in this respect.

Previous to 1914 the general policy was to use searchlights to find the target by "sweeping", each searchlight being allotted a certain arc. Directly the target was illuminated the guns opened fire; but in practice it was found that exposing the beams to find the target proved more dangerous to us than to the enemy.

The adoption of the Iris shutter enabled the light to be switched on without exposing the beam outboard until required, and the Evershed searchlight control system permitted the searchlights to be trained on the correct bearing before exposing the beam. As soon as the target reached a suitable position all that remained to be done was to give the orders "Expose beam" and "Open fire".

This satisfactory night action position was reached by 1917 and was considerably improved upon in the second World War when our ships were fitted with radar direction finding apparatus.

Appendix I

Comparative Value of W/T Direction-Finding and Aircraft-Reported Positions

Before the introduction of Radar the question of a correct assessment of the accuracy of positions given either by W/T D/F "cuts" or sighting reports by aircraft was of considerable importance to naval operations. In the case of the Italian Fleet's sortie to the south of Crete much depended, from the Italian C.-in-C.'s point of view, on his ability to gauge the accuracy of both kinds of reports and of assessing their comparative values. Our own experience of W/T D/F bearings in the Mediterranean tended to show that generalisations such as "D/F positions are more reliable than those given by aircraft" were misleading and therefore harmful. The accuracy of D/F bearings depends on a number of factors, such as the type of W/T frequency, the angle between the bearing and the coast, proximity of mountain ranges, reliability of the operator, calibration of the instruments, etc. For example, the Middle Hill W/T D/F station at Gibraltar, when on medium frequency interception, would sometimes register a difference of 15° in successive bearings of an Italian shore station. Between the bearings of 070° and 100° results were not so unreasonable, but north of 070° and south of 100° it was not found practicable to calibrate satisfactorily,[150] probably owing to interference by the Sierra Nevada mountain range to the north and the mountains of Morocco to the south. Westward, between 200° and 320°, results were better. In the Eastern Mediterranean D/F bearings from Alexandria were reasonably good, except when running parallel to the Cyrenaican coast.

In the case of positions reported by aircraft it should be borne in mind that in an area where reconnaissance takes place within only an hour or two's flying distance from land results should not be much in error, nor – in practice – were they.

On the morning of 28 March 1941 for instance, A/C B and F's reports at 0722 and 0739 were both some 12 miles to the eastward of the estimated geographical positions of Forces Z and X respectively, but a comparison of the British and Italian plots shows that quite possibly the aircraft-reported positions were more nearly correct than those estimated by the ships. Clearly, when assessing the value of sighting reports or D/F "cuts", it is necessary to treat each case on its merits, but Admiral Iachino began his assessment with a general bias in favour of D/F and so came to a wrong conclusion.

In the first case, his A/C report of 1215/28 did in fact locate our main fleet some 20 miles 040° from the correct position, whereas the 1314 D/F "cut" (if it was our main fleet W/T which was intercepted) was 100 miles 135° from the *Warspite* at that time, yet the A/C position was rejected and the D/F accepted, the assumption being that both messages came from the group reported in the 1215 message. A different sort of error was now added to the positional mis-judgment, for a wrong significance was given to the addressees of the 1315 intercept. Both the Italian Admiralty and the C.-in-C. were aware that British merchant ship traffic between Alexandria and Greece or Cyrenaica would probably be suspended after receipt of the Sunderland's sighting report of 1220/27 March. Even so, there was the possibility of a warship on passage between Malta and Alexandria, or other Eastern Mediterranean ports, which might be reporting her E.T.A. or a submarine sighting.[151] If she had come from Crete, which was quite likely, then Crete as well as Alexandria might be expected in the address of her signal. There was little ground for the assumption that "because Crete and Alexandria were included in the address the ship must have been a senior officer's ship," and therefore likely to be included in the group sighted at 1215.

So one error is piled upon another; the A/C position is rejected in favour of the D/F, the authorship of the 1315 message attributed to an imaginary authority, the two reports are considered to be concerned with the same group of ships and the false conclusion then reached that "some of the British fleet from Alexandria was at sea in a position 170 miles S.E. of the *Veneto* at 1315"; surely a classic example of a wrong decision reached from faulty reasoning, leading eventually to a major disaster.

Appendix J

Italo-German Arrangements for Air Operations in the Eastern Mediterranean 26–28 March, 1941

26 March

By Italian Squadrons

a.m. Recco. of Alexandria and Suda Bay.

By German Squadrons

p.m. Recco. of Alexandria and Suda Bay.

27 March

a.m. and p.m. Recco. between the parallels of Syracuse and Malta to the eastward of Sicily as far as 20' E.

a.m. and p.m. Recco. to the S.E. of Gulf of Taranto in the direction of 150° for a distance of 300 miles between Cape Rizzuto and Cape Santa Maria di Leuca.

a.m. Recco. of Alexandria and Suda Bay.

a.m. Recco. on the line Alexandria to Kaso Straits.

a.m. Recco. to the south of Crete

(a) p.m. Night attack on Malta airfields.

(b) Protection of the Naval forces at sea from 2 hours after sunrise till 2 hours before sunset.

(c) Striking Force of fighters to the eastward of Malta.

(d) a.m. and p.m. Recco to the eastward of Sicily between 33° and 36° N. as far as 26° E.

(e) p.m. Recco. of Alexandria and Suda Bay.

28 March

a.m. Dawn bombing of Cretan airfields and fighter protection to the fleet from 0730.

(a) a.m. and p.m. Recco. to the east of Sicily between 32° 30' N., and 35° N. as far as 26° E.

a.m.	Recco. of Southern Aegean induding Suda Bay; special attention to the area Crete-Morea-Gulf of Aegina and line joining Zea-Milo-Cape Sidero.	(b)	Fighter protection of naval forces up to 2 hours before sunset whilst westward of 21° E. and north of 36° N.
early a.m.	Recco. on the line Alexandria to Kaso Straits.	(c)	Striking Force of 20 A/C standing by in Sicily.
early a.m.	Recco. south of Crete.	(d)	

By Italian Squadrons

By German Squadrons

a.m. and p.m.	Armed recco. for the protection of naval forces in the area north and south of Crete, eastward of 22° E.	(e)	
	Bombers and Torpedo aircraft ready in Rhodes.	(f)	

Performance

Italian Machines

Type	Cruising Speed	Ceiling	Flight Period
Recco-Cant Z 501	100 m.p.h.	19,000 ft.	10 hours.
Bomber-Recco Cant Z 506	160 m.p.h.	22,000 ft.	6 hours.
Recco-Spotter-fighter. R.O. 43	130 m.p.h.	25,000 ft.	5 hours.
Fighter-C.R. 42	200 m.p.h.	24,000 ft.	4 hours.
Bomber-S. 79	190 m.p.h.	22,000 ft.	8 hours.
Bomber-S. 81	100 m.p.h.	17,000 ft.	8 hours.

German Machines

German types of aircraft in the Mediterranean early in 1941 consisted of Me. 109's (fighters) with a few Me. 110's and Ju. 88's (Bombers and recco.) with a few H.E. 111's, totalling about 200 serviceable aircraft. Their performance corresponded with similar Italian types, i.e., fighters' range of action was about 400 miles and bombers' 900.

Appendix K

Messages Before and After the Battle Between Italian and German Naval Staffs

I.

19 March, 1941.

To: Italian Naval Staff.
From: German Naval Liaison Officer, Rome.
Subject: Naval strategic situation in the Mediterranean.

    The German Naval Staff has instructed me to communicate to you the following views of the Commander-in-Chief of the German Navy:

    The German Naval Staff considers that at the moment there is only one British battleship (*Valiant*) in the Eastern Mediterranean fully ready for action. It is not anticipated that heavy British units will be withdrawn from the Atlantic in the near future. Force H is also considered unlikely to appear in the Mediterranean. Thus the situation in the Mediterranean is at the moment more favourable for the Italian Fleet than ever before. Intensive traffic from Alexandria to the Greek ports, whereby the Greek forces are receiving constant reinforcements in men and equipment, presents a particularly worthwhile target for the Italian Naval forces. The German Naval Staff considers that the appearance of Italian units in the area south of Crete will seriously interfere with British shipping, and may even lead to the complete interruption of the transport of troops, especially as these transports are at the moment inadequately protected.

II.

Rome,
7 April, 1941.

From: German Naval Liaison Officer, Rome.
To: German Admiralty, Berlin.
Subject: The Italian Naval Operation from 28/29 March 1941.

(a) A verbal report by the Italian Naval Chief of Staff, Admiral Riccardi, on the Battle of Matapan.
... Admiral Riccardi spoke to me on the results of the operations as follows:

General: The outcome of the operation was due to a whole series of circumstances unfavourable to the Italian or favourable to the British Mediterranean Fleet:–

1. The Italian sortie was based on the fact that two British battleships had been definitely reported as damaged as a result of attacks by Fliegerkorps X. This claim by Fliegerkorps X and by the German Naval Staff proved to be false.
2. (The further paragraphs of Riccardi's statement concern the failure of Fliegerkorps X to provide heavy fighter escort on the eve of the battle, the success of British air reconnaissance, the advantage that the British had in the possession of an aircraft carrier for fighter protection, reconnaissance, and particularly torpedo-bombing during the battle, etc.)

Endnotes

1. Not yet issued
2. On 13 and 14 February 1941, an Italo-German naval conference was held at Merano. Admiral Raeder, Rear-Admiral Fricke and Commander Aschmann were the German representatives; Admiral Riccardi, Vice-Admirals De Courten and Brenta, and Rear-Admiral Giartosio were the Italian. A number of decisions were taken, of which, on the German side, the most important was the provision of larger escort forces for German convoys to Libya, while the Italians requested a greater assignment of Romanian fuel oil. The Germans strongly urged a policy of offensive cruises in the Eastern Mediterranean, and Admiral Iachino, commenting on this, says:– "The insistence on this idea which the Germans later on displayed and pressed on our Naval Staff, was in the last analysis the determining cause of our operation at the end of March". In concluding his report of this conference (Note I, pp. 263-267, *Gaudo e Matapan*) Admiral Iachino states:– "In order to realise how much importance was assigned at this period by the Naval Staff to the opinion of the Commander-in-Chief of the surface forces it is interesting to note that no one asked for my intervention in preparing the arguments for discussion at the conference at Merano (no one even told me that there was going to be an Italo-German naval conference in the middle of February), and no communication reached me as to the results of the conference, not even a summary."

    From German sources there is evidence to show that the date of sailing selected by the Italians was influenced by a German report that only one British battleship (*Valiant*) was effective, the other two (*Warspite* and *Barham*) having been damaged by German aircraft attacks. (Appendix L.)
3. A.G.9 = Alexandria-Greece No. 9. At daylight 28 March the convoy again turned north and was taken over by HMS *Calcutta*.
4. G.A.8 = Greece- Alexandria No. 8.
5. For composition and names of commanding officers see Appendix A.
6. Not present in the action.
7. At Maleme, in West Crete, the five Swordfish were reduced by one which crashed during the night of 26 March. 2 Fulmars, 2 Brewsters and 2 Gladiators were also available for patrol work. (Rear-Admiral (Air) report.)
8. About 18 miles north of Athens, near Tatoion.
9. In the province of Janina, mainland of Albania, opposite Corfu.
10. For the particulars of Italian ships engaged in the operations, see Appendix B.
11. Designations in British C.-in-C.'s plan.
12. This was the 3rd Division (Force X), stationed seven miles ahead of the *Veneto* (Force Y) actual course being 134° (S. 30a).
13. Signal 1826/26.
14. One was recovered intact; the charge was 500 lb.
15. Amended later to three cruisers, R.A. (A) 28/1118 (see Appendix D.)
16. British contemporary designation.
17. Enemy 34° 16' N., 24° 10' E. *Orion*'s position 33° 55' N., 24° 10' E.
18. Italians reported contact at 0815.

19. VALF report. R.A. (A) was of opinion that 5F was reporting 3 enemy cruisers as battleships: R.A. (A) 0932/28. (R.A. (A) was right – this was Force X.)
20. At 0800 *Warspite* was about 102 miles from *Orion* according to the Diagram in C.-in-C.'s Despatch.
21. This was soon remedied, and the *Warspite* steamed as fast as, if not faster than, the *Valiant*.
22. C.-in-C.'s signal log; Maleme report says C.-in-C.'s signal was received at 1005. Signals to Maleme passed through HMS *York* (Suda Bay) which had been torpedoed on 26 March.
23. This was almost certainly Force Z, see C.-in-C.'s Despatch, para. 6:– "... this squadron (i.e., Force Z) had actually been sighted and reported by HMS *Gloucester*'s spotting A/C, but fortunately for everybody's peace of mind this report did not get beyond HMS *Gloucester*'s T.S.".
24. The German report says she was steering 300° (P.G. 32280), but this was only so between 0850 and 1035, when she altered course to 090° and at 1056 to 150° (Fig. 1).
25. See Para. 9 of C.-in-C.'s despatch.
26. The *Gloucester*'s log says "12.24 battle fleet in sight bearing 046°."
27. The *Trieste*'s estimated position at 1205 was 22 miles S.E. of this.
28. The *Valiant* did not, in fact, pass the *Warspite* as the latter had also increased speed.
29. The *Orion* sighted the destroyer screen at 1229 and *Gloucester* sighted battle fleet at 1224.
30. The signalled figures 360° were probably meant to be 160° since at 1116 the *Veneto* was engaging the *Gloucester* on a course of 160° (para. 19 of VALF narrative).
31. In 34° 5' N., 23° 58' E.
32. The *Vittorio Veneto*.
33. Actually the cruisers *Garibaldi* and *Abruzzi*.
34. For Italian ships, see Appendix B.
35. Designated in C.-in-C's plan, X. Y. Z. – see Plan 1. Force X, the 3rd Division, was in fact not so far to the westward; it had turned to the S.E. for the action at 1100 and during the afternoon remained about 15 miles on the port beam of *Vittorio Veneto*.
36. The *Formidable* had only 27 aircraft available.
37. C.-in-C.'s despatch (para. 8) "which gained a hit". R.A. (A)'s signal 1634/28 reported "possibly three hits". The hit was on the port quarter and almost certainly was obtained by the leading Albacore. The torpedo struck abreast the outer propeller, 16 feet below the waterline and fractured the port outer shaft. The *Veneto* went ahead with starboard engines at 16 knots and increased to 19 shortly after 1700.
38. At Menidi, 12 each of No. 84 and No. 113 Squadron; at Paramythia 6 of 211 Squadron.
39. 214° Kithera Light 70 miles. (From Italian records this was the *Zara*'s position, *Vittorio Veneto* at 1330 being 50 miles, 145° away).
40. At 1430 *Veneto*'s position was given as 30 miles 160° from this.
41. Statements by survivors, *Zara*.
42. Presumably on account of the damage to HMS *York*.
43. Sunset at 1840.
44. See Appendix D.52. *Barham*'s log says "1705 *Nubian* and *Mohawk* detached". At 1800 *Nubian* Bore 133° 9 miles from *Orion*.
45. Captain Mack signal 1720 – 14th D.F., *Jervis, Nubian, Janus, Mohawk*; 2nd D.F., *Hex, Hasty, Hereward, Hotspur*; 10th D.F. *Stuart, Griffin, Greyhound, Havock*.
46. C.-in-C., para. 13.
47. 1st Division – *Warspite* and *Valiant*; 2nd Division – *Formidable* and *Barham*.
48. Lieut.-Commander Bolt reported them – from port to starboard – (1) 3 destroyers; (2) 3 8-in. cruisers; (3) 1 *Littorio* battleship and 2 destroyers; (4) 3 8-in. cruisers ; (5) 2 6-in. cruisers.
49. At 1950 he was relieved by a shadower from the *Formidable*. Lieut.-Commander Bolt then made for Suda Bay. There was no moon. The harbour was full of unlighted ships

and obstructed by nets. He decided to land outside using three flame floats as a place path. A good landing was made at 2125 and the aircraft taxied to a mooring inside, assisted by patrol vessels and searchlights. R.A. (A)'s report.
50. C.-in-C., para. 14.
51. C.-in-C. Narrative.
52. Later found to be large destroyers.
53. The reason for this was not known at the time. The 8th Division (*Abruzzi* and *Garibaldi*) according to Admiral Iachino, was ordered at 1630 to leave the Fleet and return to Brindisi, and the 1st Division (*Zara*) to rejoin the *Veneto*.
54. Lieut.-Commander A. S. Bolt, *Warspite* A/C Duty "Q", signal 1914. The accuracy of this and earlier reports from A/C Duty "Q" is commented upon by Admiral Iachino, who was shown intercepted copies onboard the *Veneto*. The Italian C.-in-C. also states that:– "Truly there was a striking contrast between the information situation in which we found ourselves and that of the English, who in fact had an exact idea not only of the composition and formation of our naval force, but also of their course and speed; whilst we knew absolutely nothing of the enemy forces at sea, which were following us at a short distance." (*Gaudo e Matapan*).
55. Tracer shell.
56. HMS *Formidable*'s narrative. R.A. (A) attributed the hit either to *Formidable*'s 5A or to the second of the Maleme aircraft, but as the *Pola* was hit on the starboard side, the second Maleme aircraft, which attacked on the port side, would appear to be ruled out.
57. The *Formidable*'s narrative, para. 32. The only report received from this shadower was at 1920; at 2010 it had to leave on account of lack of petrol and managed to make Suda Bay.
58. From *Orion* 1915. "Two unknown vessels bearing 295° 10 miles" (received 1918). Appendix D.68a.
59. From A/C '5 MG', 1935. "Attack completed. Probable hits."
60. C.-in-C. narrative, para. 27 (page 46). "The 14th and 2nd D.F. Immediate. Destroyer Flotillas attack enemy battlefleet. Estimated bearing and distance of centre of enemy battlefleet from Admiral 286° 33 miles at 2030. Enemy course and speed 295° 13 knots." T.O.O. 2037/28. T.O.R. 2047/28.
61. These ships must have been very considerably astern of the Italian fleet. The report does not tally with Lieut.-Commander Bolt's report of 1912 (see S. 18).
62. "Speed was kept down to reduce bow waves". (VALF report, para. 27.)
63. 2016 A.S.V., 305° 6 miles, large vessel apparently stopped; 2027 large vessel, A.S.V., 4 miiles; 2030 stopped ship, 255°, 3½ miles. (Narrative of V.A., Light Forces, in *Orion*, and of *Gloucester*. (Enclosure No. 3, C.-in-C.'s despatch.)
64. "If this ship was the battleship, she was 'fixed' and if not it was necessary to regain touch." (VALF report.) *Ajax*'s signal of 2029 was not received by *Jervis* (Captain D. 14th D.F.)
65. The *Gloucester*'s narrative.
66. 2040 from *Orion*, "Unknown ship 240° 5 miles, apparently stopped. My position is 13° 21 miles from 35° N. 21° E." (Note: This places *Orion* in 35° 21' N., 21° 5' E. and the stopped ship in 35° 18' N., 21° E.) This signal was not received by *Jervis*. (Appendix D.75.)
67. 190° to 252°, 5 miles.
68. Narrative, VALF From the C.-in-C.'s plan and the Italian Plot they were the Italian cruisers returning to assist the *Pola*. The destroyers were then about 10 miles off, bearing about 107° from VALF
69. "Red pyrotechnic signal", C.-in-C.'s Despatch, para 17.
70. This "red light" seems clearly to have emanated from the Italian fleet or some portion of it (see infra S. 23).
71. Probably the destroyer which blew up during the *Havock*'s attack. VALF thought "it might well have been the *Fiume*". (Analysis of attacks.)

72. 14th D. F. *Jervis* (Captain D), *Janus*, *Nubian*, *Mohawk*: 2nd D.F. *Ilex*, *Hereward*, *Hasty*, *Hotspur*.
73. From *Warspite* aircraft – At 1855, enemy course and speed 300° 14 knots; at 1920, 295° 15 knots; at 1930, 230° 15 knots. (C. -in-C.'s signal log.) (See Appendix D.66, 70, 71, 74.) According to the Italian account their courses were: 300° until 1915, then 270° until 1930. 300° until 2048 when they altered to 323°.
74. i.e., from northward. (See inset on plan 1.)
75. VALF to C.-in-C. 20 May 1941. para. 10 (a), and Captain (D) 14 report, para. 2.
76. C. -in-C.'s Despatch, para. 15.
77. Plan 1. The bearing of Taranto from the position of the dusk attack was about 330°; that of Messina about 300°.
78. It seems clear that there was a discrepancy between the navigational positions of the cruisers and destroyers. Instead of being four miles ahead of D.14 at 2155 the "three unknown ships" were some 10 miles on his port bow.
79. Captain (D) does not mention the light in his report, but he made the night Alarm ("Alarm bearing 10 degrees", received by C.-in-C. 2043) which was negatived a few minutes later (received by C.-in-C. 2246).
80. C.-in-C.'s Despatch, para. 17, "there seems little doubt... that this must have been the remainder of the Italian fleet."
81. 2312 "All forces not engaged in sinking enemy retire to the north-east."
82. Captain D.14 report says he altered course to north-east at 2330 (p. 258). This seems to be a misscript for 2320, for his signal to the C.-in-C. is timed 2322 (received by C.-in-C. 2325). Reply from C.-in-C. 2326 "after your attack" (received 2337).
83. See page 63 (*Ajax*'s 2029/28).
84. 40°, i.e., to course 280°.
85. Reported by *Formidable* to be the 3rd ship in the line, i.e., *Fiume*, but held by C.-in-C. to be the *Zara* (see Appendix C).
86. At 2228 (*Warspite*, p. 168), range 2,900 yards; the *Valiant*'s 7 seconds later, *Valiant* gives time of *Warspite*'s opening fire as 2226.28 and of herself 2226.35 (p. 181). *Valiant*'s time was apparently 1m. 32s. slow on *Warspite*.
87. *Warspite* narrative, p. 168, also survivors' report. See, however, C.-in-C.'s remarks (Appendix C). *Formidable* narrative says the third ship (i.e., the *Fiume*) was illuminated first.
88. According to some survivors "Within fifteen minutes, burning furiously"; according to others "There was an explosion and she sank." A heavy explosion was seen by the battle fleet at 2300 (C.-in-C., p. 47); another explosion occurred at 2314 which appears to have been the destroyer which blew up after action with the *Havock*. About 2330 the *Havock* saw a "large cruiser burning fiercely fore and aft and obviously about to blow up."
89. The *Fiume* received two broadsides from *Warspite* and one from *Valiant*. *Zara* received four from *Warspite*, five from *Valiant* and five from *Barham*.
90. The *Warspite* narrative (p. 167) "White, red, white vertical, flashing." *Barham* narrative (p. 175) "White light and made a challenge by red Very's light."
91. Rear-Admiral's narrative (p. 164) "*Barham* fired two salvoes at the leading enemy ship, 6-in. cruiser". (Note: This was later considered to be a destroyer.) *Barham* Gunnery Record (p. 180) says "Opened fire 28m. 50s. 3,100 yards, left hand ship *Zara*."
92. Some 62 15-in. shell fired at her, of which about 20 hit. Rear-Admiral's narrative, p. 164.
93. See Appendix H; Admiral Iachino explains why the Italian Navy previous to Matapan did not arrange for night firing by the larger calibre guns (*Gaudo e Matapan*).
94. At 2243 from Captain (D) 14 (negative received at 2246) and at 2245 from VALF, evidently referring to the red light seen at 2240. (See S. 23.)
95. The *Greyhound*'s report.
96. A "large single funnelled destroyer", probably the *Carducci*..

97. The *Stuart* in her report mentions sighting "undamaged cruisers". Survivors state there were no other cruisers with them. The C.-in.-C. considered "the presence of undamaged cruisers in the area at that time as unlikely".
98. Possibly the leading destroyer engaged by *Barham*.
99. Query, the *Fiume*, which from adduced evidence sank about 2300/28 March.
100. Query, the *Zara*.
101. The *Pola*.
102. No position was made and the time was given as 0020.
103. "Immediate. My 0020. For 'one *Littorio*' read 'one 8-in. cruiser'. Heavy cruisers were in the vicinity. My position 036° MB, HS 59. Am returning to shadow." (See Appendix D, Nos. 94 and 95.)
104. C.-in-C.'s despatch.
105. They may well have been the vessels which the *Havock* thought were cruisers.
106. *Griffin*'s report.
107. Greek destroyers picked up 110 survivors on 29 March. The Italian hospital ship Gradisca picked up 13 officers and 147 men between 31 March and 2 April, all survivors from the *Zara*, *Fiume*, *Alfieri* and *Carducci*. Those from the *Pola* were rescued by our destroyers. A number died from exposure on rafts but the greater proportion of casualties, which totalled about 2,400, occurred as a direct result of our battleships' devastating gunfire.
108. In 35° 23' N., 21° E.
109. Appendix D.2.
110. British terms used by C.-in-C., Mediterranean.
111. This appears to be a misprint for 190°.
112. In *Gaudo e Matapan*. N.B. Force "D" reported four Ju. 88's passing overhead at 1405/28, when patrolling west of Kithera Channel. Ju. 88's and Me. 110's were both twin-engined low-winged monoplanes, but the latter had twin rudders (S. 28).
113. p. 136, idem.
114. p. 307, idem.
115. See Appendix I.
116. Probably *Havock*. *Havock* gives time as 2345.
117. Probably *Greyhound*, but *Griffin* gives time as 0141.
118. HMS *Jervis* gives time as 0325.
119. Captain D. 14 says:– "At 0340 I cast off and put one torpedo into *Pola*. As she appeared to be settling very slowly, I ordered *Nubian* to fire a second which finished her off."
120. About 2330, the *Havock* saw "the burning wreckage of what could have been a cruiser or destroyer. There were a large number of boats, rafts and survivors in the water and the last remaining vestiges blew up shortly afterwards."
121. The survivors thought she had been scuttled, attributing her destruction to scuttling charges about 0200.
122. i.e., at 0956 (S. 9).
123. Idem para. 10.
124. This "heavy fighting" must have been the various engagements of the *Stuart* and *Havock*, *Griffin* and *Greyhound* with escaping destroyers (325).
125. C.-in-C.'s Despatch, p. 5, para. 17. Admiral Iachino remarks that at about this time he made repeated attempts to communicate with the *Zara*, so that it is more than likely the *Veneto* fired a red pyrotechnic signal to indicate their position.
126. 10 Albacores, 4 Swordfish.
127. "Unable to keep up" 0.834/28 (VALF Narrative). Ordered by C.-in-C. to proceed independently to Alexandria.
128. Designation as given in Plan 1.
129. Sunk.
130. Full name is *Luigi di Savoia Duca Degli Abruzzi*

131. From Italian account this was almost certainly the destroyer *Alfieri*.
132. Note: Later considered to be a destroyer (see C.-in-C. supra).
133. i.e., the leading destroyer (see above).
134. C.-in-C. signal 0906/29; R.A.'s Narrative (para. 9) states also that *Griffin* drawing ahead across line of fire was straddled by a 6-in. salvo from *Warspite*, but received no damage.
135. This was the *Pola* (R.A. Narrative, p. 164).
136. i.e., turn together 40° to starboard.
137. Leading enemy ship 6-in. cruiser. (R.A. 1st B.S., Narrative, p. 164.) Note – Later thought to have been a destroyer. (C.-in-C.'s Despatch, p. 5.)
138. i.e., *Fiume*.
139. This may have been the *Havock* (C.-in-C.'s signal log, 0906/29) (p. 80).
140. *Warspite*'s track passed through 103 GV FR 17 at 0700.
141. Apparently misscript for 303 GV FR 100 = 33° 56' N., 24° 21' E.
142. cf. No. 7, *Orion*'s position.
143. Naval Base in Greece, near Piraeus.
144. This was Force Z, the 2 *Garibaldi* cruisers being mistaken for *Cavour* b.s.
145. (sic) probably for "North West".
146. Destroyers.
147. Query 2129.
148. Note – That is to 240°.
149. At 2220 *Greyhound* and *Griffin* were ordered to take station on the starboard side of the battlefleet. *Greyhound* was slow moving over and received a "hastener" (2224) from the C.-in-C., who records that a minute or two before opening fire "*Greyhound* wasn't anything like half a mile ahead, she was right in the line of fire..."
150. An exhaustive series of trials was carried out and an official report made, from which the above figures are quoted from memory.
151. The destroyer *Vendetta* was approaching Alexandria, but did not make her E.T.A. signal until 0015/29. The C.-in-C. Mediterranean made a signal at 1318 to the *York* and F.A.A. at Maleme (2 addressees) ordering the dusk torpedo attack on enemy forces. If this latter was the signal intercepted then Admiral Iachino was right in assigning the origin to the same group as sighted at 1215, but wrong in his implicit faith in the W/T D/F "cut".

HRH Prince Philip

HRH Prince Philip of Greece and Denmark joined the Royal Navy in 1939. As a Special Entry Cadet, who had completed his schooling at Gordonstoun, he should have gone straight to sea in a training ship, but the ship was in refit so by chance he found himself at Britannia Royal Naval College, Dartmouth. Here he was to excel as a cadet, being awarded the King's Dirk for the top cadet in his entry. He was also able to spend time with his future wife, during a Royal visit in July 1939.

At the outbreak of World War II, Prince Philip was still a Greek citizen, but it was decided he should continue to serve in the Royal Navy. His war got off to a slow start. In January 1940, he joined the battleship HMS *Ramillies* as a Midshipman and spent the following six months in the Indian Ocean, also serving on HMS *Shropshire* and *Kent*.

In October 1940, Italy invaded Greece and Prince Philip became a combatant. In January 1941, he joined the battleship HMS *Valiant* in Alexandria. It was on board *Valiant* that the Prince became a participant in the night action off Cape Matapan, and was mentioned in despatches for his control of the midship searchlight.

On returning home, Prince Philip qualified for promotion to Sub-Lieutenant, before being appointed to the destroyer HMS *Wallace* based at Rosyth, for convoy escort duties on the east coast. He was promoted to Lieutenant in July 1942 and in October, at the exceptionally young age of 21, he was appointed First Lieutenant of *Wallace*. In July 1943, *Wallace* took part in the Allied landings on Sicily.

After further courses, he was appointed as First Lieutenant of the new fleet destroyer HMS *Whelp*, which joined the 27th Destroyer Flotilla and sailed for the Indian Ocean to join the British Pacific Fleet. *Whelp* was in Tokyo Bay when the Japanese signed the surrender and Prince Philip continued to serve onboard *Whelp* until she returned home in January 1946.

In 1949, after instructing at the Petty Officers' School and attending the

Naval Staff College at Greenwich, Prince Philip, now a married man, was appointed First Lieutenant of HMS *Chequers*, Leader of the First Destroyer Flotilla in the Mediterranean Fleet, based at Malta. He was promoted to Lieutenant-Commander in 1950, then appointed to command of the Frigate HMS *Magpie*.

In 1952, he was promoted to Commander, but his highly successful naval career ended with the death of his father-in-law, King George VI, and he retired from the Royal Navy in 1953. He was made Admiral of the Fleet on the coronation of Queen Elizabeth II. In 2011, the Queen appointed him Lord High Admiral on the occasion of his ninetieth birthday.

Dr J. E. Harrold

Dr Jane Harrold is Deputy Curator of the Britannia Museum at Britannia Royal Naval College, Dartmouth. She joined the College from the University of Warwick in 1997. Her PhD thesis was entitled *State Building: The Case of the EU's Common Foreign and Security Policy (CFSP)*. It examined the evolution of CFSP and its implications for the future of European integration and state provision of security. Her teaching and research interests continue to include the evolution of the EU's Common Foreign and Security Policy, in particular European Security and Defence Policy, contemporary security studies and twentieth century international and naval history. An enthusiastic supporter of European co-operation, Dr Harrold has presented papers at the Ecole Navale and for the Franco-British Lawyers' Symposium at the Ecole Militaire.

Additionally, Dr Harrold is the BRNC Archivist – she was involved in setting up the Britannia Museum. In 2005, she co-authored, with Dr Richard Porter, a definitive history of the College, *Britannia Royal Naval College 1905–2005: One hundred Years of Officer Training at Dartmouth*. For this, they were awarded the Sir Robert Craven Trophy by the Britannia Naval Research Association. A revised, updated edition was published in 2007 as *Britannia Royal Naval College, Dartmouth: An Illustrated History*; reprinted in 2012. Dr Harrold has also contributed to *The Naval Review* and to TV programmes, making a number of media appearances herself.

Britannia Naval Histories of World War II

Never previously published in this format, documents once stamped 'secret' have been sourced from Britannia Royal Naval College's Library. These include reports and plans drawn up by serving Royal Navy Officers during and immediately after World War II. BRITANNIA NAVAL HISTORIES OF WORLD WAR II also contain Germany's recorded view of action against the British, with Hitler's comments, as they were typed and filed at the time: the Fuehrer Conferences.

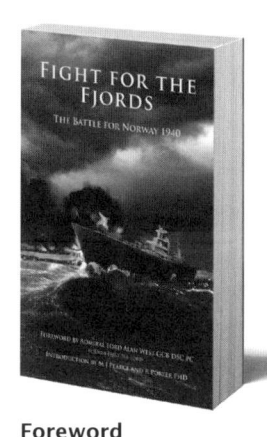

Fight for the Fjords
The Battle for Norway 1940

The fierce naval battles fought in Norwegian waters during the spring of 1940 were recorded in documents that were once subject to restrictions under the Official Secrets Act. *Fight for the Fjords* includes the German account, written within three years of the end of World War II, and the British report, which compiled previously unavailable Royal Navy records to produce one complete account. The combination of these two summaries forms a unique record.

Paperback
ISBN 978-184102-306-9
Hardback
ISBN 978-184102-305-2

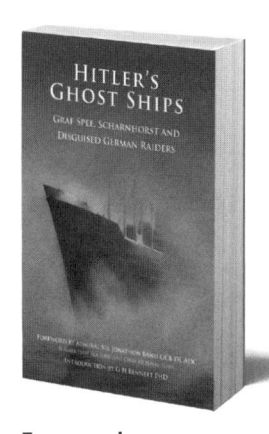

Foreword
Admiral Lord Alan West, a former First Sea Lord and Parliamentary Under-Secretary of State at the Home Office

Hitler's Ghost Ships
Graf Spee, Scharnhorst and Disguised German Raiders

Disguised Auxiliary cruisers could sidle up to merchant vessels undetected as they were flying a neutral flag, similar to 17th century pirate ships. Completion of the disguised ships was difficult and took its toll on the German dockyard workers and crews, sailing in waters dominated by the Royal Navy. The Battle Summaries chart how the Royal Navy dealt with the threat of these raiders of 70 years ago.

Paperback
ISBN 978-184102-308-3
Hardback
ISBN 978-184102-307-6

Foreword
Admiral Sir Jonathon Band, former First Sea Lord and Chief of Naval Staff

Hunting Tirpitz
Naval Operations Against Bismarck's Sister Ship

While it was the RAF that delivered the final *coup de grâce*, it was the Royal Navy, from 1942 to 1944, that had contained, crippled and neutralised the German battleship in a series of actions marked by innovation, boldness and bravery. From daring commando raids on the coast of France, to the use of midget submarines in the fjords of Norway and devastating aerial attacks by the Fleet Air Arm, the Royal Navy pursued *Tirpitz* to her eventual destruction.

Foreword
Admiral Sir Mark Stanhope, First Sea Lord and Chief of Naval Staff

Paperback
ISBN 978-184102-310-6
Hardback
ISBN 978-184102-309-0

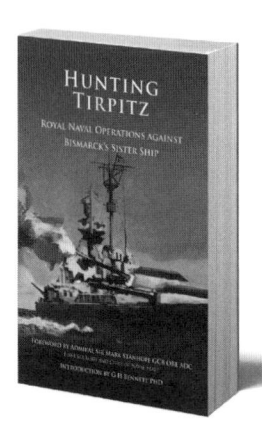

Bismarck
The Chase and Sinking of Hitler's Goliath

Launched in 1939, Bismarck was the most formidable surface ship in Hitler's fleet. Sunk on her first and only war cruise, 27 May 1941, this great victory for the Royal Navy was also a human tragedy. Only 114 of her 2,200 crew survived the Royal Navy's final storm of shells and torpedoes. The complete Battle Summary is included, detailing how Hitler's Goliath was located, pursued and attacked. Both German and British first-hand accounts embellish the turn of events.

Foreword
Commander Nigel 'Sharkey' Ward

Paperback
ISBN 978-184102-326-7
Hardback
ISBN 978-184102-327-4